Ascending to 1st Chair: A Lesson in Leadership and Organization Development

By

Tom Kaden and Michael Gingerich

Foreword by Garry Ridge, Chairman Emeritus WD-40 Company
& *The Culture Coach*

Mark,

Someone To Tell It To
Harrisburg, PA

Values matter!

Michael Gingerich & Tom Kaden

ISBN (Hardback): 979-8-9850344-3-1
ISBN (Paperback): 979-8-9850344-6-2
ISBN (eBook): 979-8-9850344-4-8
Library of Congress Control Number: 2023902140

Cover Design by Russ McIntosh
Book Interior Design by VisionIdeaDesign

Printed in the United States of America

DISCLAIMER

The Symbol

The Listener's symbol

is intended to remind each of us

to take time out of our day

to *see* the faces and *listen* to the voices of

the people we lead,

not only with our ears,

but also, with our hearts.

And to realize that

they are our most important

resources and relationships.

To The Some*Ones* We Love

To everyone whose stories inform our message, vision, and values.

To our team members whose undergirding of those values makes their impact greater.

To Sarah and Kathy, and the families we each share with them, for whom the legacy we hope to leave will make life more beautiful.

We must value people first. If we don't value our team members for simply who they are, not what they produce, people become a means to an end (and not the end). People aren't robots, people have deep emotions, perspectives, attachments, and personalities.

Tom Kaden and Michael Gingerich
Co-Founders and Co-Chief Listening Officers
Someone To Tell It To, Inc.

FOREWORD

Many years ago, I was given the privilege to lead the "tribe", the community that is the WD-40 Company. Our tribal culture is the secret to our success, it is our "secret sauce."

I learned a long time ago that you can't make anybody do anything and sustain it if they're not passionate about it. You can pay them money to do things for a certain period of time. But if there's not a real purpose and a real passion in what they want to do, people sit and quit.

Look at what's been going on in the world the past few years. They call it the great resignation. I'm calling it the Great Escape. People are escaping toxic cultures because they're just not putting up with the sort of environments that they're going to work in every day. But there is an antidote to this problem:

Belonging. Love. Friends.

This is where all the benefits of employee engagement begin. Simply put, when individuals feel supported, accepted, proud of their colleagues, safe to be themselves so they can focus on their work, rather than squander their energies on internal politics, they can invest in who they are in the mission of delivering their best work. But historically, companies haven't given themselves the chance to intentionally create a culture that promotes those feelings of belonging. The trend toward developing emotionally healthy company cultures is slowly emerging now. And those of us who have gone ahead on this journey owe it to the workplace world to help show the way.

Acceptance and belonging have been the key all along by defining mutual agreement around values, practices, mission, purpose, and ways of doing things. As I wrote about in my most recent book, *The Unexpected Learning Moment: Lessons in Leading a Thriving Culture Through Lockdown 2020:*

"Once we are accepted into the group, we trust each other. We share knowledge freely and openly. We always assume the best of each other's intentions. We sacrifice for each other. We celebrate with each other. We honor our contributions as individuals without losing sight of the valuable, positive impact on the entire community. While no organization can achieve this state constantly or without being tested, our objective is to work toward achieving this condition at least 95% of the time."

Leaders have to love their people enough to ensure that they're rewarding and applauding them for doing great things. Genuinely modeling these qualities makes leaders great. They lift everyone in the organization, which makes the organization great.

If you are a leader in any organization, this recent work by Tom and Michael—*Ascending to 1st Chair: A Lesson in Leadership and Organization Development*—is for you. It can help you to achieve your tribal culture 95% of the time. In it, Tom and Michael offer a valuable message about having strong values within your organization and living those values through everything you do.

The organization that Tom and Michael created and lead—Someone To Tell It To—is a global leader in the growing listening movement. The values they model and teach through their organization are very much in sync with the values that I did my best to model at WD-40 Company—empathy, authenticity, respect, belonging, affirmation, gratitude, humility, vulnerability, compassion, love, and a lot of listening. People who feel listened to and more connected with others in their lives can find their stress levels and blood pressure lowered. Incidences of burnout and feeling overwhelmed decrease.

Ascending to 1st Chair: A Lesson in Leadership and Organization Development encompasses those values and shows us how leaders can learn and grow in their personal development to influence and nurture others in theirs. The result is organizations that become great because of the way they serve to make this world a better place.

This book shows us how.

Garry Ridge

Chairman Emeritus, WD-40 Company and *The Culture Coach*

Our values are what unite us; they bring us together in a protective eco-system of our day-to-day work and decisions. Values also set us free. They are the guidelines which, once learned and embraced, release us to focus on the activities that make us successful—both as a tribe and as individuals.

Garry Ridge, Chairman Emeritus, WD-40 Company and *The Culture Coach*

PROLOGUE

Jaime entered the building that morning on a mission. She spent the previous evening tossing and turning, planning how she would approach Jeffrey with the news. The past ten years were filled with growth and learning, experiencing frustrations, learning to manage her reactions, moving up the ladder of success, and celebrating accomplishments. All this, with no regrets. When she commits to something, she commits.

The heavy glass doors she entered daily seemed lighter, matching her mood and her resolve. For several months she recognized her need for change. She wanted something that would help her transform and be challenging. Her husband Freddy, always the encourager, played the devil's advocate as she shared her desires for something new with him. He posed every possible question and scenario to dissuade her instincts.

Their daughter kept asking if Jaime would be home more often if she changed jobs and if they would be able to visit *Nonna* and *Nonno* in Italy for longer time periods. Of all the scenarios and questions Freddy asked as Jaime sifted through this decision-making process, Luna's was the most heart-wrenching because she had to answer *no* and give an explanation followed by a promise. A promise she would do everything possible to keep.

This is how Jaime's transformation happened.

One day an opportunity presented itself when a friend told her about a startup that was struggling to grow. The business succeeded through the first three years and experienced revenue growth and consistent prospective client inquiries. They were finding it difficult to scale and keep up with demand. Jaime's heart pounded as her friend told her about the founders and the team. She could feel the excitement resonating and knew what to do.

She clearly remembers one week after learning about the position. It was her day off, and she woke up feeling renewed and got dressed as if she were heading to the office. In the living room she set up the phone, the green screen, and a comfortable chair—one on which she would not slouch. The company did not request a resume or a list of references. All they wanted for the first phase of the interview process was a video and social media account handles. She picked up the list of questions and hit record. After finishing, fearing she would delete the recording if it were edited to satisfy her need for perfection, off the recording went after hitting send. She sent it out to the cyber-universe and the owners, then forgot about it. This was the first sign that change was coming. Whatever happens, will happen. A sense of peace befell her. What she just did was not her usual *m-o*.

Two weeks after submitting the video the invitation for an interview arrived. The day of the appointment, she dressed in her best suit, signature four-inch heels, made sure every strand of hair was in place, and her make-up impeccable. She left an hour early because she is always prepared. The metro stopped and she moved toward the exit with the usual cosmopolitan array of people wearing everything from blue jeans and sneakers to Armani suits. They moved in unison, the doors to the train opening and the rush of subterranean air whooshing in then retreating, pulling all who needed to exit out with it.

As she left the station she stepped on unfamiliar turf. The buildings were low- or mid-rise and there was a lack of glass structures, save the large windows of the warehouses-turned-office space. Taking a deep breath, she checked her phone for walking directions and with one foot in front of the other, began a new phase in life by agreeing to be interviewed for the position of CEO for a tech startup.

The sliding door to the right of the newly installed glass entry was a nostalgic reminder of what used to be in place here. It was a former textile distribution warehouse. The lobby was bright with artificial light and the person at the reception desk may have been older than Jaime. She told him the company she needed to go to, and he called to let them know she was waiting in the lobby.

Next, she heard footsteps on the metal stairs and found herself shaking hands with someone who looked like she could be young enough to be her daughter. Her goth-like style gave Jaime a jolt. She hoped the shock that gripped her internally didn't show on her face. Francis was the COO of the startup and would be the one conducting the interview.

They made their way to SpecialMe.org's section of the coworking space, three offices separated from the common area by glass panels. She noticed the casual nature of everyone and immediately felt overdressed and uncomfortable. "I have the conference room reserved," Francis explained. "It's around the corner."

They sat in ergonomic seats at a long table. The decor was reflective of the socially conscious businesses occupying the spaces and the value of community and collaboration. Again, she felt like this may have been a bad idea.

They talked for over an hour. Francis explained that they loved her video because they could tell it had not been edited. "We want authenticity here. It's one of our core values." Their creative minds fed off each other, and by the end of the interview a rough outline of how the business could evolve was developed. The whole process was amazing, invigorating! Jaime could have stayed the rest of the day. There did not exist a care in her mind if they took the ideas, used them, and did not offer her the job. The interview validated her need for change. Now her mind was churning with possibilities for growth. She was alive with anticipation and could visualize a new world for herself and her family.

A week later, Francis called to offer Jaime the position. They discussed when she could start.

And this brings the story back to the present. Today she needed to tell Jeffrey she will be leaving in two months.

"Good morning, Jaime. How are you?" Jeffrey left his seat at his desk and, in his new signature move, greeted her warmly and gestured for her to sit in one of the two chairs that were facing each other.

He really has changed, she thought to herself. Just two years ago he was on the border of being a tyrant. She still had some residual fears from that era and could not help but wonder if old Jeffrey would come back for a visit after hearing her intention to move on to a new opportunity. He had worked with two Listeners who helped him implement a new way of communicating using the L.I.S.T.E.N. acronym. Lean In and Remove Barriers, Interested and Curious, Simplify and Self-Care, Talk Less and Embrace Silence, Explain and Ask Questions, and Negotiate the Win/Win.

She had to admit L.I.S.T.E.N. was a method she felt she used instinctively. But it was not until Jeffrey modeled this method of communicating and interacting, then helped others put it into practice, that she realized that she needed some refining to be a more effective leader.

"Can I get you anything?" Jeffrey asked, waking Jaime from her thoughts.

"No, thanks," she replied, immediately realizing her mouth was dry and regretting the response.

"I hope you don't mind. I'm going to finish my smoothie. My wife insists I have one a day to stay healthy," he laughed. "Not sure that it works but it can't hurt, right?"

All Jaime could do was nod and look out the window.

He noticed her discomfort, a skill he developed since starting his transformation and meeting with the Listeners. Today, in Jaime's discomfort and anxiousness about the announcement, she found his insightful disposition a little annoying as he sat across from her and took a sip of the smoothie. He did not say a word. Jaime looked around the office and out the window for what seemed an eternity.

Thirty seconds had passed, and she blurted out, "I'm leaving." It was a bit curter than intended but she saw no other way to do it. Always putting others first was Jaime's default. So was being dedicated to this company. So, declaring her intent to depart felt like the equivalent of ripping a Band-Aid off, fast with a stinging effect.

He just stared at her waiting. "I need a change. I've felt this for a while. I have hit a ceiling and need to break through. To do this, I need to move on."

Jeffrey listened patiently, nodding his head, leaning in, hearing every word she spoke. Once she was finished, he asked, "Is there anything else?"

"No, except to say I feel so relieved. I haven't had the courage to make a change. Being comfortable is within my wheelhouse. I don't rock the boat. I keep the peace. So, this is a big step. I appreciate all you've done for me and all that we've accomplished together. It's just time for me to move on."

"I agree."

She was astonished! He sat back in his seat nodding his head, agreeing with her.

"I've seen it for a while. As much as I want you to stay, I can't keep you here. It's not fair to you or to this company. Selfishly, it's not fair to me either. I have come to rely too heavily on you and, if I'm going to grow, I need to let you go and bring someone new on board."

Her mouth was hanging open. This was too easy. *What's the catch?* she kept asking herself cynically. She feels cynicism but rarely shows it publicly. But today she was annoyed and cynical. She thought he would beg her to stay!

"Well, thanks Jeffrey. I appreciate your candor," she finally declared, trying to suppress the cynicism. "I guess we should discuss my exit plan."

"Agreed, again. Where are you going and when do you start?"

They leaned toward each other, both interested in the process of change and not talking over each other except out of sheer excitement for what the future might hold. They developed a two-month exit plan which included Jaime interviewing the people who would replace her and Jeffrey having the final say.

Deep down, she could not wait to leave. Her professional side reminded her that she could not leave without fulfilling her duties to the people with whom and the company with which she had been engaged for the past ten years. Still, she wanted to put on some skates and headphones, roll out of the office and around town shouting, "It's my time!"

Back home that evening, Jaime, Freddy, and Luna were preparing to attend a youth orchestra concert. Luna was learning to play the violin and they tried to take her to as many orchestra concerts as possible to keep her motivated. She told Freddy about her conversation with Jeffrey and admitted she was slightly disappointed when he supported her decision instead of asking her to stay.

"This is going to be different, for both of us," Jeffrey chimed in. They stared at each other with a little bit of fear in their eyes. This was new and they would have to adjust.

"I suppose it could be worse. One of us could have lost our job. I know it will be an adjustment, but we'll be fine." With that, Jaime hugged Freddy and left the room to check on Luna.

At the concert, there was a new person sitting at the front of the U-shaped orchestra. He sat to the left of the conductor. This was the person who ascended to first chair of the youth orchestra after several auditions. Jaime watched the orchestra conductor emerge from behind the stage and command the attention of all who sat before him once he reached the podium. Throughout the concert, Jaime admired how the conductor brought the music to life, how the instruments were expertly manipulated by the musicians to evoke emotions. The young musician who occupied the first chair for the strings section kept watch in a mysterious way over the orchestra as the music filled the auditorium. It was a magical lesson in leadership and team development.

How the conductor accomplished this intrigued Jaime. She wanted to take the time to meet him when the concert was over, but Luna was exhausted. On the way home, Jaime told Freddy about her revelation and how she hoped, as a new CEO, to be able to bring that type of fluidity and harmony to the organization.

Little did she know that her path would cross that of the orchestra conductor sooner than anticipated.

You do not think yourself into a new way of living as much as you live yourself into a new way of thinking.

Fr. Richard Rohr, Center for Action and Contemplation

CHAPTER ONE
Welcome to Your New Role

Three months into the new job and Jaime was starting to feel some tension and frustration. The honeymoon was over and real conversations had to be initiated. She was in regular contact with her former boss, Jeffrey, who offered her as much guidance as he could. But with the recent hiring of her replacement at Tandem, his time was limited.

She was gaining a profound appreciation for the responsibilities of a CEO. She never questioned Jeffrey and was passive when making observations about the stress a CEO had to endure. In three months, she was exposed to more than she anticipated. To top it all off, her struggles stemmed from a steep learning curve since she had never worked for a technology company, let alone a startup.

The Founders

SpecialMe.org was in its third year, having experienced profit and growth since year one. The founders, Francis, Mitchell, and Katrina, tapped into an underserved community and chose it as the focus of their social mission. SpecialMe.org developed software to support the needs of youth and adults with physical, emotional, and cognitive challenges.

Francis, the COO, and Mitchell, the Chief of Human Resources, met while volunteering for the Special Olympics. They shared concerns, struggles, and a strong desire to help because both had family members with disabilities. Francis's younger brother was diagnosed with learning challenges in kindergarten and then Asperger's just before he entered ninth grade. Though high functioning, his social skills at that tender age put him in precarious situations because he could not tell the difference between sincere kindness and bullying. Her strong inclination to protect him from others laid the foundation for her commitment to combat misperceptions, insensitivities, and pure ignorance about the challenges of people on the margins and those facing the most severe challenges of the autism spectrum.

Mitchell's father is blind and a single parent. He lost his mother when he was two years old after she was struck by a drunk driver. His father is his hero and their extended family indispensable. From as early as age five, he accepted the responsibility of helping his father negotiate the seeing world. He never missed a meal with him. As a teenager and now, as an entrepreneur, he is finding solutions to help those who are blind from birth, disease, or accidents so they can assimilate with their surroundings.

Katrina did not have the experiences and challenges Francis and Mitchell lived with all their lives. She is a professed free spirit with a need to solve the world's problems. This sometimes gets her into trouble—social unrest, consciousness-raising events, and civil disobedience are part of her DNA. As a trans-woman, she knows firsthand the feeling of being the "other." She has been fighting for LGBTQ+ rights since her teenage years when she told her family her deepest need in life— to live authentically. At 32 years old, she is still moving in the direction of full transformation. Money is always a primary consideration when making her plans. Insurance covers some of the surgeries, but she still must save to pay a substantial portion of the cost out-of-pocket.

Francis and Mitchell met Katrina at South by Southwest in Austin, Texas. They stopped to listen to her contemporaneous presentation on Diversity, Equity, Inclusion, and Belonging for

LGBTQ+ youth on social media. They were immediately drawn to her passion, commitment, and novel concepts. She had a plan to impact the lives of the people she represented using financial literacy and social media. What she did not have was the knowledge to create backend coding. They all agreed this is where Francis and Mitchell could fill the gap. Their partnership was formed, and a business was created that addressed all their life missions as one.

For three years they worked remotely, meeting once a year for one week in person. They worked on software to meet the needs of people with learning challenges and disabilities and developed a social media presence that targeted the LGBTQ+ community and financial literacy. Over the course of their fledgling years, they talked about discrimination in the workplace and the lack of opportunity for those with disabilities. They met with insurance company representatives to discuss policy, and they never missed an opportunity to engage people at the local supermarket.

They developed ideas for entrepreneurial endeavors and created an online Chamber of Commerce-like organization. Financial literacy courses were developed, workshops that engaged employers about the value of hiring people with disabilities were presented, and podcast invitations flowed in.

Slowly during their second year, they started to hire employees who would help with software development, technology, and selecting hardware to support their needs. Their first two hires were Larry who works remotely and has been blind since birth, and Kristofer who is a veteran and wheelchair-bound because of injuries he sustained when deployed. They became the frontline workers who served not only as technicians but also in customer relations. When followers and participants reached out with questions, they took it upon themselves to answer each immediately with solutions, to let followers know that they would do the research or give them a resource better suited to answer their questions.

Everything seemed to be moving forward smoothly when they received an offer to buy their business. They had many long discussions about the pros and cons of accepting the offer. This included conversations about what they thought would happen to the business if they let it go and what they could do if they kept it. Larry and Kristofer were part of the discussion since they would be impacted too.

During a heated discussion, Larry pushed his bottle-thick glasses up on his nose and peered into the camera. He told them about a program he was developing to help homeschooled children with physical and learning challenges. He was still testing it with a few local families and homeschooling co-ops, but seemed to be moving in a direction that was beneficial. "What do you think about expanding?" he suggested.

"I don't know," chimed Katrina. "What we are doing for a community I'm passionate about is proving to be effective. I don't know if I wanna veer away from this and add another aspect. Who would manage the new program?"

Larry gave her a look as if to say, "Me, of course."

"I get it, but we need to think bigger. Plus, what Larry is suggestin' allows us to expand our service to a community we all know and understand. Even you know about the physical and learnin' challenged and autistic community now, Katrina, since you've worked with us for the past three years," Mitchell pointed out.

"Still, I don't know. The offer to buy the company is fantastic and the buyer is reputable," Katrina retorted.

They all sat in silence for a few minutes just staring at each other on their respective monitors.

Then Francis spoke up, "What if we keep it, expand our capabilities to serve more communities in need, and hire a CEO to help us negotiate the expansion?"

"That's a tough ask," Mitchell said. "We've been runnin' this company for three years and experienced success since year one. Now we're talkin' about expanding our service, a software development project, *and* a new person?!" His exasperation was palpable. "I just don't know. Honestly, I don't know if I'm willin' to give up control. I can get on board with helpin' another community— obviously I got a vested interest in that—but addin' another person as CEO. I jus' don't know."

"I have to agree with Mitchell," Kristofer's New York-accented, deep bass voice finally piped in. "I'm all for expanding our reach and who we help but I'm not necessarily sold on the concept of bringing in someone new. We have a close group here, a great working relationship. What would a new person do to this?"

"I just want to point out that when we started this company, we committed wholeheartedly to three of our tenets: opportunities for those on the margins, open and inclusive communication, and supporting the Special Olympics," Francis reminded everyone. "I think we've done this well so far. But maybe we've reached a plateau and need help to clarify our mission, remind ourselves of our vision and values, and discover how to climb the next mountain. Just a thought."

They sat in silence for a few more minutes then finally decided to take a couple of days to think about the discussion. They would reconvene Thursday with the intention to decide whether to sell or hire a CEO and expand. Francis contacted the company interested in buying them out and told them they would know the decision by Friday.

Back to Reality

Jaime sat at her desk and started doubting her decision to take on this challenge as CEO. It was the first time she had a tinge of regret. She joined SpecialMe.org and hit the road running, full speed ahead. She was the crescendo for the orchestra to embrace, join, and follow. After the interview, it became clear that they needed her expertise. *Needed* being the operative word in her mind.

As the past three months progressed, the strength, determination, foresight, and expertise of the founders and the team slowly began to strip away her confidence. She tried to force her ideas on the team because she was the *most experienced*. She dismissed the input of others as naïve and not in congruence with *her* plan. Before she knew it the chatter started, the cold shoulders, heads bowed down staring at the table or phones or other screens during the weekly meetings, and the enthusiasm and energy that was prevalent when she started began to wane.

"Good morning," Francis stood at the entrance to their shared office. Today she wore all black with a red belt. Her platform boots had studs along the back. "Let's take a walk and get some fresh air."

Jaime was a little taken aback by Francis's sense of authority. *She* was the CEO now. How could the COO take such liberties and suggest they take a walk? But she could not say no, so she shook her head as she stood and did not make eye contact until they were sitting on a park bench with warm beverages in hand.

"What's up?" Jaime asked in her perkiest voice and Italian accent, which was always more prevalent when she was anxious.

"Well, it's been three months since you started here. How do you think we're doing?"

"Things are great, don't you think?" Jaime retorted with great confidence.

"Hmm. Well, let me ask you this. What would you consider our greatest achievement since you joined us as our CEO? Three months may not seem like enough time to give an assessment, but in this business, time doesn't stand still. This business moves, as Bill Gates pointed out, at the speed of thought. So, tell me, what have *we* accomplished to grow the business?"

Jaime noticed the emphasis on *we* and was taken aback. *We* and being inclusive has always been her method of functioning at work, home, and when volunteering. She has always insisted on being inclusive in thought and action. But today she was clearly hearing that she was not practicing this way of being at her new place of employment. "Why are you asking me this?" She was in a defensive posture now.

"Let's come back to that," Francis calmly guided Jaime back to her original question.

"Let me think about this. I hit the ground running and thought we were doing productive work." Emphasis on *we*. "But let me think this through. Do you need an answer right now?"

"I think it's best to work in the heat of the moment sometimes. So, yes, let's talk about this right now. This isn't an interrogation. It's a conversation. I want to learn from you, and, through our discussion, I hope you'll learn from me." Francis sat back and crossed her studded platform-toting legs, then covered them in modesty with her black, ground-length coat.

"Okay. Well, um, let's see. I established a weekly meeting on Mondays so we're all on the same sheet of music. I've reached out to clients to introduce myself. I've reviewed the financials and presented a plan to increase revenue. And let's see . . . I, um."

"That's great. We've seen that too and agree it has helped the company. But what have *we* done?" Again, there was an emphasis on *we*.

"I'm not following. I've made every effort to include everyone in the conversations and planning. It's part of how I function and fundamental to my beliefs."

"Trust me, that's one of the reasons we offered you the position. That and your experience as the Senior Vice President at Tandem. We recognized we needed more structure and analysis of the company's systems and processes to move toward building a sustainable business. And, to date, we believe your expertise has put us on the right path. So, let me ask you this. You believe in the concept of "we" at work, yet in response to my question about accomplishments, even though I asked for *our* accomplishments, your response had only "I" statements. What do you think about that?"

Jaime had to take a deep breath. Using "I" in her response seemed natural. At her old job, she would have never used I-statements. She thrived on team accomplishments, collaboration, and the input of others. Where did this person come from who seemed to not listen to others?

"I can't respond to that right now. Am I doing that consistently?"

"Let me answer that with another question. Since arriving have you seen a change at our weekly meetings?"

Jaime's eyes darted back and forth as she scoured her memory to find the chronological pictures of the meetings to help her respond. She crossed one leg over the other, exposing from beneath her fashionable pants suit the signature four-inch heels that helped her rise from 5'2" to 5'6". This was not an attempt to establish presence but a part of her Italian couture culture she wholeheartedly embraces. Her personality, confidence, and competence were fully on display when she worked, defining her leadership style, and establishing her credibility.

"Francis, this is a lot for me to absorb. I need a couple of days to think about what you are asking. Is that okay?"

"Absolutely. Let's plan to continue our conversation this Friday. As a matter of fact, let's make this a weekly end-of-the-week meeting."

They walked back to the office. Jaime had to admit that she was a little uneasy and confused. Not just about the conversation but also about the question of using *I* and *we*. If there was anything she prided herself on while at Tandem, it was her ability to build teams and collaborations. Now all of this was being challenged. What had changed?

Each of us has twenty-four hours every day. But it's what you do with your twenty-four hours that makes a difference.

Mary Kay Ash, Founder, Mary Kay, Inc.

CHAPTER TWO
Paradigm Shift

Jaime and Francis returned to their co-working space. Normally Jaime would be in high spirits, walking in with a little bounce as her heels clicked on the polished, concrete floor. This time she walked a few steps behind Francis attempting to hide from her coworkers and even the other people who had desks or offices in the building. She felt as though they all knew about the conversation she and Francis had and were judging her.

Walk the Line

Sitting at her desk around noon, Jaime finally pulled up a blank document on her computer and started writing. Accomplishments—me/we. Ideas—me/we. Lessons from Tandem—what worked there/what works here. SpecialMe.org—how it functions. SpecialMe.org—what it needs. SpecialMe.org—what works well/what needs to improve. SpecialMe.org—strengths/weaknesses. SpecialMe.org—what distinguishes what we do from other small tech companies. Me—what have I forgotten to do and why/how to assess and refocus. Me/We—mission/vision/core values.

For the next hour, Jaime filled in her assessment. At the end of it, she formatted a blank document and attached it to an email for the team with this message:

Hello Team!
I hope all of you are having a great day! Let me start by saying thank you for all you have done to keep our company moving forward and growing.
I've been working on the attached document for the past hour or

so following a conversation with our COO, Francis. I think it's
important for all of us to create beautiful music together to be
satisfied professionally and to build a sustainable business that
serves our stakeholders today and into the future.
Would each of you please take time this week to review the
document and answer the prompts? We will discuss this at our next
meeting. Plan on attending a two-hour meeting so we can discuss
current needs and then move on to this document.
From "I" to "We"—let's move forward.
Jaime

It's Okay to Ask for Help

After Jaime hit the send key, she picked up the phone to call Jeffrey, her former boss. His phone rang two times before it went to voicemail.

"Hi, Jeffrey. It's Jaime. Wondering if you have time for a quick call or to meet for a cup of coffee this Saturday. Give me a call. Hope we can meet. Thanks."

There, it was done. She knew it was a critical moment in her professional life and she needed advice. Jeffrey was the only person she could think of whom she trusted to give her sound guidance. She waited anxiously to hear from him.

While she was in a meeting with clients, Jeffrey called and left a message.

"Jaime, sorry I missed you. It was great to hear your voice. I'm sure you are having a profound impact at SpecialMe.org. I'm available Saturday but it will have to be around 6 a.m. I have plans with the family for the day. If you don't mind, I'm going to invite a couple of friends to join us. I think they will be great sounding boards. I'm taking a leap of faith here based upon our previous conversations. Let me know if this works. See you Saturday."

Jaime replied by email this time and Jeffrey sent her a calendar invite. Exactly who his friends were piqued her curiosity. This was going to be a great week now that she had Saturday to look forward to.

An Encounter at Home

"I'm meeting Jeffrey at 6 a.m. Saturday."

"Really? What for?" Frederick, Jaime's husband, was a little annoyed with the announcement. Since taking the position of CEO, he had not seen her on weekends, which was out of the ordinary for them. While at Tandem, Jaime had time to spend with Freddy and their ten-year-old daughter, Luna. This change in career affected their relationship and his reliance on Jaime to be available. Luna was becoming somewhat withdrawn, spending more time in her bedroom than she did with the family.

Dinners were a little tense because the topic of discussion revolved around Jaime's new job. Freddy and Luna were becoming cogs in a wheel, cardboard cutouts who joined her at meals and when she decided they fit into her schedule. Several times over the last three months Freddy tried to talk with her about their home life. Each time she explained that she was in transition, had to learn about the company, and promised things would get better.

They were still waiting for things to get better. Instead, Jaime seemed to become more and more immersed in the new role and company.

"You seem anxious, baby. What's wrong?" Jaime tried to pull Freddy in close and was shocked when he turned away.

"We're good. Thanks for letting me know about the meeting. We'll just leave for our trip a little later." With that, he walked out of the room towards Luna's bedroom to let her know.

Dinner was uncomfortably quiet. When Jaime tried to ask how the day went for each of them, she received a one-word answer, "Fine."

Her heart broke and she was confused by this shift in character and family dynamics. When did this happen? Why did this happen?

"Thank you both for understanding about my meeting Saturday. I really appreciate both of you."

"No worries," Freddy replied. With that, he and Luna began clearing the dishes from the table, cleaning the kitchen, then going their separate ways.

Jaime could not move.

Listening is fundamental to good leadership and management; however, to be effective, it must be practiced with great intention.

Rosalind G. Brewer, CEO, Walgreens Boots Alliance

CHAPTER THREE
Meet Your Listeners

Jeffrey called early in the morning to let Jaime know he would not be able to meet with her and the Listeners. "I'm sorry to have to do this, but I can't meet with you and the Listeners this morning. It's probably better this way. I won't be in the mix, the conversation, bringing up my point of view. You'll get fresh ears. I promise they›ll be great and so will you," with that he laughed heartily, and they said *see ya*, their normal departure sentiment.

Jaime stepped off the metro and was confronted by a crisp fall breeze. The day started with a wonderful breakfast made by Freddy, bacon and eggs for Jaime, and pancakes for Luna. They even managed to do more than smile at each other by using conversation starter cards. It was a new tactic that Luna suggested they try. She was a special ten-year-old. A little too mature and prescient for her age. Somehow, she always captured emotions before they were expressed and diverted interactions toward something positive. It was an amazing experience.

This morning she cornered her dad and insisted he make breakfast for all of them, because she was, "Starving!" For dramatic effect, she grabbed her stomach and bent over, feigning passing out.

Jaime smiled as she pushed through the chill and recalled the morning's smiles and laughter. It was a twist in the current state of affairs at the Douglas home. She wanted to bottle up that sense of joy to be able to open it and drink from it any time she started to become stressed or worried. For now, she had to settle for the short-lived happiness of that morning's breakfast.

She agreed to meet the Listeners at a local co-op. Jeffrey had reserved a meeting room for one hour. They were not allowed to bring in food or drink, so Jaime was even more grateful for the breakfast she had eaten that morning. Once she reached the entrance, she entered the code and hurried inside the historic building. Up the steps she flew hoping to warm up. As she turned the corner, she spotted the people sitting in the windowed room. They were not what she expected.

"Stop anticipating, Jaime. Stop judging. This isn't who you are," she kept this mantra throughout the meeting.

Strategically seated facing the hallway to see Jaime, when they saw her, both stood as she entered the room. "I'm sorry I'm a little late," Jaime puffed out as she caught her breath from running up the stairs. "Wow! I guess I need to get in shape. Those steps were hard." Everyone laughed politely, her Listeners glancing at each other.

Liam O'Connor spoke first after they settled at the table. "Jaime, it's a pleasure to meet you. We've heard so much praise about you from Jeffrey." His Irish accent filled the air between them with joy. Jaime thought he looked familiar.

"Thanks for meeting me. I hope Jeffrey didn't reveal too much about me," she laughed, a little nervous.

"No, don't worry. We always arrive with a clean slate in mind," Maria Sanchez assured her. "We're here for you, today and throughout the time we meet. Until you're ready to move forward without us."

"Thanks. That's reassuring because there may be a lot to unpack. Even more than I anticipate." Jaime settled back in her chair, her signature 4-inch heels now a part of a cold-weather ensemble. "How do we start?"

"That's up to you. Jeffrey told you a little about us, right?" It was Maria posing the question.

"Not really. I did have your names, so I looked both of you up on LinkedIn and did a Google search." Jaime squirmed in her seat uncomfortable with that admission, feeling like a stalker, but knowing this was common practice in today's tech-driven world. "Also, I know you're from the same organization that helped Jeffrey and introduced L.I.S.T.E.N. to him."

Maria caught the discomfort and laughed a full belly laugh. "Oh my gosh! Don't even worry about looking us up online. Do you know how many people I 'research' online daily?" Maria used her signature, as Jaime would come to know, air quotes when she said research. "Just about everyone I encounter, including you."

Jaime could not help but smile as this vibrant twenty-something entrepreneur helped her relax. "With social media being an omnipresent tool, everyone lives in a glass house nowadays." This time she ended her comment with a tone of caution.

"I'm learning all about that at my new job. I thought I understood technology and social media. Little did I know the creative genius behind the development of all of it. The people I work with are teaching me so much."

"Trust me, technology has permeated the music world for years, decades, in fact. But there is so much more to keep in mind. A lot of challenges, even for me," Liam added.

Jaime looked at Liam, trying to place him. His profile picture on LinkedIn looked familiar and she knew his profession. But it still was not registering why he looked so familiar.

The Listeners

Liam O'Connor emigrated to the United States in 2000. He arrived with a green card in hand because his name was selected from the green card lotto. He applied for this opportunity in 1997, '98, and '99. The beginning of the new millennium proved to be his fresh start and opportunity to fulfill his dream to become an orchestra conductor.

"We share that in common," Jaime declared with a vibrant smile. "I moved here when I was young. Though I have dual citizenship, American and Italian, I spent the better part of my youth in Italy. My father was in the U.S. Air Force and stationed in Italy when he met my mother, who is Italian. We stayed there as long as possible until the Air Force decided it was time for my father to return to the U.S. I was about 15 years old and almost bilingual. I spoke nothing but Italian at home and, of course, in school and our community. I knew many words in English, but it was terrible when we arrived and, just like today, I had a thick accent."

"I feel you," Liam responded, using popular vernacular he adopted over the years. "It was hard to adapt and overwhelming. I moved to Boston thinking I would be welcomed because of the large Irish population. But it proved to be more uncomfortable than comfortable or comforting. Even what was considered traditional Irish food tasted a little different or was prepared differently. I had a lot to learn."

"I understand. Living in the D.C. area, my parents thought I would assimilate quickly. But even in a place known to be multicultural, I found it hard to adjust. Plus, I had to learn to speak, read, and write English with fluency."

They laughed and turned to Maria who was nodding her head knowingly. "I didn't emigrate to the U.S., but I am the first to graduate from college. I grew up in a small Texas border town where the schools were not that great. I'm bilingual, too, though you wouldn't realize it because I have an American accent. I had to battle the misperceptions not only of someone like me with my heritage, but as a young girl interested in technology, coding, math, and entrepreneurship. Thankfully, I had a great teacher who took me under his wing and together we developed our first app, entered a tech competition, and then built a small business around it. We're still partnering today."

"Good golly! How old are you?" Jaime could not stop herself from blurting out a question she would have found offensive.

Maria smiled. "I'm twenty-four."

Jaime was stunned and confused. What could a 24-year-old teach her?

Maria continued, "I'm asked this all the time. Let me explain one thing. I've been in business, in one way or another, since I was 16 years old. I've been developing software programs since I was 13. Technically, no pun intended, I've been in business for eleven years."

Jaime had nothing more to say. She was silenced by her Listener's qualifications. All qualifications that were not available by taking a course online or attending a seminar. Maria earned her degree from the school of hard knocks. "I guess you never really know about a person until you choose to listen to their story," Jaime confessed.

"Oh my gosh! That's a page out of our playbook," Liam declared. "Arrive with an unassuming mind. We must dump all our assumptions and judgmental tendencies to be able to hear and listen with an empathetic and compassionate disposition."

Jaime could not help but like the two of them. Relaxing, she found herself leaning forward to soak in all they had to share. She did not reveal much about herself and her situation. They did ask questions for clarification. But this was a time for simple conversation, which was nice and unexpected.

Liam checked his watch. "It's almost time to go. So, tell us, would you like to continue meeting?"

"Absolutely." Jaime could already feel some of the pressure of her new job easing. Her chest did not feel as tight, and her mind was less foggy. "I can't wait. How does this work?"

"We'll meet with you regularly. Because we all work, it's best to find a day of the week and time that works for all of us. Is that okay?'

Jaime nodded and Maria added, "How long this takes to help you work through whatever you need to talk about is up to you. We'd like to recommend meeting once a month. Does that sound reasonable?"

"Yep. It's probably best. We have a lot of changes going on at work. Quick question," Jaime looked at them slyly. "Will there be homework?"

They all laughed. "The only homework will be whatever you decide to do. We're here first and foremost to listen. We both have expertise in our given professions from which we can pull and serve as guides, if you want this."

Jaime knew she wanted their help but did not understand how they could help. "So, can we start by meeting once a month for three months then reevaluate?"

"Absolutely. This is all about you and what you need. Shall we schedule our next meeting?"

Jaime reached for her spiral-bound calendar. She glanced at them expecting a reaction. Even without seeing one she felt compelled to say, "Old school, I know."

"Whatever works," Maria reassured her.

They set their next appointment and agreed to meet at the library for the next three months. "Text me and Liam if you need anything in between our meetings," Maria explained as she sent her contact information to Jaime's phone and Liam did the same. "We'll start a group text."

"Thank you for meeting with me today. I'm looking forward to seeing the two of you next month." It was obvious Jaime's mind had shifted to her daily to-do list. Her posture closed in, head was kept down, and the speed of her movements increased as she gathered her phone, purse, and briefcase. She blindly waved goodbye and turned to walk through the glass door. Practically running in her 4-inch heels, she made a beeline for the steps then disappeared.

Probably one of my best gifts was being able to understand creative talent: how it behaves, how to bring |the most out of it, how to manage it.

Jann Werner, Co-Founder, *Rolling Stone*

CHAPTER FOUR
A Conversation with the Team

Jaime walked into the office feeling rushed. The week before she had met with her Listeners and absorbed their conversation gaining confidence that she could do the job as CEO. But the past week proved to be a challenge. Though she thought she was implementing the L.I.S.T.E.N. method effectively, something was being lost in the execution.

There was no or slow response to her emails. Phone calls were placed on hold. Face-to-face conversations seemed to be lacking. She tried engaging the team when they were on their conference calls but was greeted with tops of heads and profiles by the participants who seemed to be busy with other things and not paying attention. And no one was providing feedback. She could not figure out what was going on.

The team had had their discussion about the questions she had posed in her email. It was positive and productive but not necessarily effective. Change for her personally and for the organization was a slow process. She had to learn how to be patient since she had never led a group of people through a transformation and scaling plan. Her learning curve was steep.

She texted Liam and Maria to ask if they could have a quick call. Following the conversation, she decided it was time to be a little vulnerable with the team. If one of the values of SpecialMe.org was open communication, it had to include being vulnerable and not always being "the boss." She spoke with Francis about her idea, and they put it on the calendar.

Today was the day of the meeting, and Jaime felt ill-prepared, nervous, and not feeling like today was the best day to be vulnerable. She wanted to put on her boss-lady shield and forge ahead through the day. Unexpectedly, she received a text from her Listeners: *Champions choose the difficult over the easy. It's the only way to improve and realize their vision.* They were paraphrasing the author Jim Afremow who wrote *The Champion's Mind.*

She chose to face her fears. Today they would begin a conversation on values. It was developed by the company the Listeners represented using the word as an acronym with a twist: *L.I.S.T.E.N.—Values.* They would use as a guide what was shared by the Listeners but fill in the shared values they want for SpecialMe.org.

Jaime was extremely nervous. Her experience was as a participant. On the rare occasion, at her old job, she was the facilitator, she always knew she had someone else to blame if things went south. Namely, her old boss. That realization was an epiphany she did not anticipate. She always considered herself to be cooperative and a supporter. Not someone who would seek out a scapegoat.

Today, she had to realize that if she did not set the tone, someone working here could decide to make her the scapegoat for their failures or lack of effectiveness. Facilitating shared values was one step towards bringing the team together and helping her feel like a part of the organization.

Letting Go of the Past to Embrace the Future

Everyone was on time. She found a minute to gain some composure and strength before entering the virtual meeting. She smiled and welcomed everyone then asked, "Would all of you please close whatever you have open—books, computer screens, but not this one, and silence your phones. Better yet please put your phones on silent *and* out of sight. If you need to, turn off the Bluetooth connection so your watches won't buzz."

While everyone complied, she took a few deep breaths and prepared mentally to facilitate the discussion. "Thanks for cooperating. I want to start with this, today is an opportunity to start fresh. I have been drinking from a fire hose since arriving and am trying not to drown." There, she did it, the first declaration to show she is not a super-CEO.

"Well, the honeymoon is over, and I need your help. It's not only for me, but for all of us. We need to define who we are as a team, an organization, and members of our community. Today, all I'm asking you to do is listen. Simply listen. Listen to each other as we begin to assess where we are in our industry, as a company, and with our stakeholders. I can't think of a better way to start than with a discussion of our shared values for SpecialMe.org."

Silence. Blank faces staring back. Utter silence.

Jaime took a deep breath and continued. "Okay, I'm the new kid in the group. And, as the new kid with my perceived maturity and depth of knowledge because of my experience, I've tried to implement a structure, system, and mindset that is a remnant of my past. I'm ready to let that go, fully accept, and adapt how we function here to become a part of the team."

Some started to shift in their seats and lean in. Others remained stoic. Predictably, her one ally, Francis, smiled.

"We're only going to take an hour today. I've got an agenda but want to open the mic for any comments. I guess," she sighed, "consider this an opportunity to air your concerns. I can put the agenda to the side and bring it back next week."

That opened the door and the little yellow hands started appearing on the screen, participants asking to be heard. Jaime, sporting her armor but with her shield down, let them speak.

She simply listened.

Listening is done with more than our ears. We hear words, but we must attune ourselves to our partner's tone, striving to capture the intention beneath the word. Using our intuition, we may discover a very different message than the words convey.

Julia Cameron, Author

CHAPTER FIVE

Diabetes, Health Insurance, and Being the Primary Breadwinner

Jaime arrived home late again. This was becoming a common occurrence just like working through the weekend. She never seemed to catch a break. Exhaustion was overtaking her. To top it off, Freddy was growing distant. When she tried to speak with him, his response to her was limited to either a nod, a shrug, or one word. It was all a veiled attempt at appearing to listen. There was always something in his view that served as a distraction, so he didn't have to look up, like a newspaper, his phone, or the laptop. Jaime was growing weary and worried.

Tonight, she chose to confront him. In an accusatory tone she asked, "What is going on? Every time I come home you barely acknowledge me."

After hearing the desperation in her voice, he looked up, captured her eyes, and spoke. "It's not me, honey."

"What is that supposed to mean?"

"It's not me. I'm here. I wait for you every night to come home and every weekend to squeeze us into your schedule. I put Luna to bed every night reassuring her that you'll give her a kiss as soon as you come home." His deep voice somehow made its way from her ear straight to her heart and soul, stinging instead of soothing her anxiety.

"I don't understand. I'm trying to do everything. We agreed when this opportunity arrived that I would work, and you would cut back on your contracts and be home for Luna. Our ability to continue to afford our lifestyle depends upon my job." Her Italian accent rose to the surface thicker than the usual lilt she had developed over the years when she spoke English. Her passion for all things danced with her hands, facial expressions, and Italian words that punctuated her state of being.

Freddy sat silently allowing this incredible woman, whom he loved, the space to have her say. After fifteen years of marriage, he knew this was the time to listen. But in the back of his mind, he wondered if she would do the same when it was his turn. "Is it possible," he thought to himself, "that I have created this form of communication by not insisting that she also listen to me?"

As he watched his wife wind down, he knew it was time for him to assert his needs in the conversation. "Jaime, I've been very patient and listened to every word you've said. Not just today but through the years. I've always thought that we've been pretty good in our communication. But today, I have to tell you, I'm beginning to think I'm not being heard. Do you take into consideration what I may need?"

Jaime took a sharp breath. He had never asserted himself in this way. She always relied on him to be her sounding board even when they had discussions like this. All she could do was stare at him as a little bit of anger welled up but remained under control.

He saw her eyes narrow, her fingers grip the countertop, and the fact that she was holding her breath. Freddy sat up taller on the stool, gaining confidence. Then his baritone voice came forth, "I'm not complaining. I know what we have agreed to do, and I support your dream. But don't you see me anymore? Don't you recognize what I do in support of our family? All I hear about is your work. You've missed several of Luna's school events and we've canceled weekend plans too often."

Jaime took a step back. This was easier to experience without bringing Luna into the conversation. She looked down, shaking her head. Tears were on the brim of her eyes, and she began to sniff.

"Please don't do that," Freddy stood up and walked toward her. "I really need you to listen. I'm not trying to make you cry. I'm trying to tell you what I need and how I'm feeling right now." He gathered Jaime in his arms, and she welcomed his embrace.

"Don't know how," she finally declared.

"Don't know how to *what*?"

"I don't know how to listen to you. I rely on you to always be available for me when I get home. This isn't an easy position to be in. I feel the stress of needing to make sure we can go to the doctor when we need to, that you can get your insulin, and that there is food on the table. I feel like I don't have time to think about anything other than work."

"Trust me, I know." Freddy tried to laugh but was hurting inside and wondering if this was a good time to have this conversation. "Maybe we can talk about this tomorrow."

Jaime thanked him and turned to go kiss Luna goodnight, then go to bed.

Freddy stood in the middle of the kitchen, head hanging, heart heavy. Jaime had changed since taking the new job. He anticipated some changes, but this was different. She was less attentive and more distracted. They both had demanding jobs before she accepted the CEO position and he agreed to be a stay-at-home dad. He had cut back on the consulting contracts and rearranged all his meetings to make Luna his priority. But he felt distant from his wife and wanted to go back to the way things were. He knew this was not an option because she truly loved what she was doing, and he recognized that she was growing and thriving. Still, it was a difficult change.

Now the question he had to ask himself was whether he would continue the conversation in the morning. Could he? Or would he let this slide and just accept it as a necessary means to an end? But what would the end be?

Jaime looked in the mirror and the streaks on her face. She was still in shock and a little heartbroken knowing that Freddy was not happy. How can she fix this? She could not imagine her life without him, that simply was not an option. What needs to happen? She was not a fan of the notion of work-life balance but had to admit that following their discussion, maybe there was something to it. "He wants me to listen to him," she whispered to her image in the mirror. "I used to listen. Why is there a different me today? Is it the new job?" More questions swirled through her mind as she prepared for bed. She could not help hoping the conversation would not continue in the morning.

Breakfast was quiet. Each ate their usual meals and then did their part to clean the kitchen. It was a Saturday morning and Luna was waiting for her friend, Serena, to arrive so they could spend the day together at the zoo, then a sleepover at Serena's house. When she finally gave her parents a hug and the door closed behind her, Jaime and Freddy watched from the window as she jumped into the minivan all smiles and laughing with her favorite bear firmly held in her hand.

"Well, shall we continue our discussion?" Freddy asked in Italian signaling the need for a deep conversation.

Jaime stiffened but knew they had to. "Sure," she answered warily.

"I know you may be uncomfortable with this, J," his shorthand for Jaime always warmed her heart. They sat across from each other, and Freddy took her hand. "Listen, I'm not asking you to quit your job. I see how much it means to you. All I'm asking is that you make some time for us and yourself. I see how tired you are when you get home. I worry about your health. Can you sustain this tempo?" He was doing it again, making the conversation about Jaime and not getting to what he really wanted to talk about.

Jaime looked a little uncomfortable and wanted to pull her hand away. She felt selfish at that moment, but she pushed through it. "I'm at a loss for words. What do you want me to say? Am I tired? Sure. This isn't an easy job, especially since I'm new to this industry and they function a lot differently than I'm used to. I've only been there about four months now. I just need you to give me a little more time to adjust."

With that request, Freddy could not hold back anymore. "I understand your need to adjust," his voice was terser than he intended, and he had let go of her hand while sitting up straight. Jaime's tears started again. "Please don't cry. I'm trying to stay calm but it's hard." He choked up a little.

"Just hear me out," he continued, in Italian, not giving Jaime a chance to speak. "I just need to be reassured that we're still at the top of your list of things you value. I need to know that your career isn't going to get in the way of us, that I won't be pushed aside. Sometimes it feels like you use your work as an excuse to not be with us." Jaime tried to interject at this point and Freddy raised his hand to stop her so he could finish.

"Jaime, just listen." She nodded and took one of his hands in hers as he continued. "This is what I fear, your schedule will become so full of things to do with work that you won't be able to fit us in, not because you don't want to but because the expectation you have set at work is that you're always available. Do you understand what I'm saying?"

Jaime nodded but did not say a word.

"All I'm asking you to do is, starting this week, block off time for our family. Block off time for just the two of us, and time for yourself. The sooner you do this, the better our life will be in the future. Does this make sense?"

Jaime was not sure if the question was rhetorical or if this was an invitation to join the conversation. She looked at Freddy trying to figure out what to do.

She got her answer when he continued. "I sit at this table every night wondering when you're going to come home. I sit at school events hoping you'll walk through the door. I cringe when I hear your phone vibrate. I don't want this to continue." With that, Freddy tried to discreetly wipe tears from his eyes. His shoulders slumped and exhaustion took over.

All Jaime could do was hold his hand and let the silence envelop them. It was awkward yet comforting.

"Freddy, I didn't realize that all of this was living inside of you. I thought you were okay with my schedule and pace and lack of availability. I didn't know."

"I know, Jaime. I've been trying to keep things going. This has been a difficult transition for me too. I'm used to working full-time and splitting the responsibilities at home. With your old job, our old way of living, we seemed to have more time for everything. Now, you're not available. I'm trying to be patient but it's not easy."

"Wow. I seriously didn't consider this as a transition for you too. I thought you would be fine, and everything would fall into place without a hitch. I just didn't know."

They spoke for a few hours. The tension eased as one listened to the other and affirmed what each was experiencing and wanted to change or incorporate into their family routine. Jaime didn't try to sugarcoat what she would do. She was honest about the challenges of being a CEO and needing to find balance (there was that work-life balance concept again). She explained to Freddy her responsibilities and committed to ensuring time with him and Luna was always on her schedule. She asked if he would give her at least a month or two to get it right, to which he agreed.

Accountability became part of their family values. They committed to keeping each other in check, to listen not only to words that were said, but also to be conscious of body language and what was being left unsaid.

Time and choices were on their side. Putting the plan into action would be a challenge but one they are willing to face together.

Then Monday arrived.

The triumph can't be had without the struggles.

Wilma Rudolph, Gold Medal Olympian, Rome 1960

CHAPTER SIX
L.I.S.T.E.N. - Values

Jaime's first meeting with her Listeners was the Monday following her eye-opening discussion with Freddy. She was running late and barely made it to their agreed-upon location, which moved from the library to the cafe in a local museum. She saw them seated at a table by the window and practically ran in her four-inch heels toward them, waving her hand and apologizing profusely.

"I'm never late. But for some reason I seem to be late when it's time for us to meet," she puffed out as she sat in the surprisingly comfortable standard plastic chair. They were by the east-facing window that let the sunshine through, warming their small corner of the cafe.

"Not to worry. We've been here only a few minutes and haven't ordered anything yet. The server left a menu for you," Liam reassured her.

"You look fantastic," gushed Maria. "I love your shoes. Wish I could wear heels but those would put me over 6 feet tall!" She laughed at the thought of her towering stature. "On second thought, in my business that might not be a bad thing."

They all had a good laugh at that. Liam stood about five feet six inches tall. Next to Maria, who is 5'10" and a former volleyball player, they made quite a pair. Laurel and Hardy-ish and just as amusing. They certainly knew how to play off each other. An amazing team.

Jaime told them about her time at work following their initial meeting and then explained what had happened at home. "I must admit, I'm a little nervous talking about this. Not noticing people and not listening is out of character for me."

"Hmmm. Maybe I can chime in here before we talk about values," offered Maria. "When I was in middle school, I was already 5'9". Everyone thought I would go on to play basketball. I had no interest in basketball," she declared emphatically. "All I wanted to do was play on my computer. But I did like volleyball. So, I talked to my parents about it, and they agreed to help me find a volleyball team to join. There weren't any in the town where I lived. It turned out I would have to change school districts for high school. My parents did everything they could to move me into a district where I could play volleyball and continue my first love— writing code.

"I had relied on my parents for everything. They taught me how to work hard and not limit myself to what others thought I would be capable of doing. I listened to them and always wanted to make them proud and happy. But then the time came when I was doing well in volleyball and developing my computer skills, as well as my self-confidence. Suddenly, it seemed, my parents weren't enough. I stopped hearing what they had to say. Their advice didn't matter anymore. I thought I knew better and that everyone else was smarter than my parents.

"In my sophomore year, my computer programming teacher and I developed a new app that grew in popularity so quickly I couldn't keep up with anything. My grades started to slip. I missed practice, and I was never home.

"I thought I was a rockstar. Then one day I got a call from my mom. My dad was in the hospital. All kinds of emotions filled my body. You see, I was at a volleyball tournament in another county about two hours away. What was my first thought? It wasn't that I wouldn't play. It was *Can I play and then go see Dad?* I chose the latter to my mother's surprise. I told her I'll be there as soon as the game is over. I didn't tell anyone on the team, not even my coaches knew. I didn't want them to know because they would have sent me home.

"You see, I thought I could do it all on my own. I didn't think my parents, who were my catalysts and biggest supporters, needed me. I played the game, went home, and found out my father needed heart surgery. My mother had to endure that news alone."

Maria took a deep breath and continued, "Even though I chose the latter, my mother held no grudges. When I arrived at the hospital and saw her sitting there, obviously crying, I sat down next to her and she took my hand and said, *'He's going to be okay.'* My father could have died while I was playing volleyball. I chose my team over my family. In that moment, I had clarity. It was the first time I considered what I truly valued in life. In that moment I knew family was everything to me."

Jaime sat dumbfounded as a woman, approximately thirteen years younger, taught her a fundamental lesson. Life is short, your family will always be there, and everything else is temporary. She had no retort.

"Think about what Maria just shared, Jamie. It isn't the same as your conversation with Freddy, but the lesson is relevant."

"I know, I get it," was all Jaime could say.

They ordered lunch and ate while they discussed the topic of the day.

"We advise organizations who are trying to incorporate listening as part of their DNA. It's not an easy thing to do because everyone from the CEO to the janitor must embody it. You know this because of your experience at Tandem Corp. But what needs to be included as an organization moves in the direction of transformation, growth, even rebranding is a solid definition of values.

"We have used L.I.S.T.E.N. to define a method of communication and as our acronym to define the company's values. It may not be the right acronym for your company, or even your family, but it serves as a guide to put organizations on the path of defining this integral part of who they are and why they exist."

Liam pulled out a small envelope and pushed it across the table like he was sharing state secrets. It was a little humorous. Before Jaime took it, she did the obligatory sideways glances to make sure no one was surveilling them. Then she slipped it onto her lap and as secretively as possible opened the envelope. They got a good laugh out of that.

"We've never had anyone consider our documents to be as important as state secrets," Maria laughed.

Jaime set the paper on top of the table and unfolded it. L.I.S.T.E.N. in bold letters was laid out at the top of the document. The subtitle read, *What We Are, Strive For, and Do.* Underneath each letter was a visual representation of the word chosen to define each value. *L* - Luminaries. *I* - Impassioned. *S* - Service. *T* - Teamwork. *E* - Excellence. And *N* - Notice. With each word was an explanation of how the organization embodies and practices their meaning.

"As you can see, Jaime, we have taken a lot of time to consider each word in our acronym. This is not something that can be done in a few hours. An exception may be if you have values defined and are revisiting them to make sure they are relevant and being practiced," Liam's Irish accent almost made it sound as if what he had to say came straight from the annals of ancient times. Jaime leaned in so she would not miss a word.

"We don't know how much Jeffrey shared with you about the process, so we are going to tell you how this works," explained Maria. "Each month when we meet, we'll discuss the L.I.S.T.E.N.– Values acronym. Notice that that is only six months' worth of discussion. Don't worry, we've got the remaining four covered."

"Four?"

"Yes, four. Today is the first meeting of twelve. The final meeting will be a closeout one. That leaves us with four. Sound good?" Jaime nodded and Maria continued. "Each time we're together it will be in person unless we have to meet virtually. If a virtual meeting is necessary, we'll provide the link by email. It's imperative we commit to monthly conversations. If you need to reschedule, we ask that it be within the same month. Liam and I will be with you every step of the way."

Jamie said she understood and then asked, "How long is each get-together? What if the conversation isn't about a set topic? For example, what if I have something pressing I need to discuss?"

"Great questions," Liam piped in. "Because we all work, we have a structured meeting. We meet for one hour and make every effort to respect your time. We understand that sometimes we need to discuss something other than what is planned, or we may go over an hour. If the topic changes, we have a little flexibility to move it to next month. However, for our purposes and knowing you'll still be building your CEO confidence, we'll try to keep you on track. If the meeting exceeds one hour, don't worry. Maria and I always set aside two hours. But we want to be conscious, as I said, of your time and schedule."

Maria picked up the explanation, "Our intent is to model the L.I.S.T.E.N. method of communication by allowing you to speak more than we do. It may not feel that way to start. In this type of engagement, we may have to speak more than anticipated to be able to explain a concept or give an example.

"We have become experts at asking questions, some that'll make you a little uncomfortable but have the intention of helping you move in a positive direction and to grow. We include, because we have found it to be necessary, some consultation. Let me explain the distinction between three of our services.

"If you were a person in need of someone to simply listen because you are in distress, suffering in some way, and only need someone to listen to you, then our purpose is to do just that. We simply listen. We offer guidance and ask questions with the expressed purpose of helping a person heal and be able to move forward with their life.

"Then there is the training we offer to corporations, nonprofits, and other organizations in need of improving their form of communication. With our training, we serve as facilitators. Our purpose is to improve listening skills, teach the ability to discern when someone simply wants to be listened to and doesn't need anything fixed, from someone who may need a little more guidance and conversation which could include mentoring, coaching, and/or training and development."

"Finally," Liam now, "there is the service we are providing for you. It's also training on listening but includes aspects of coaching and consulting. We work with seasoned CEOs or, like you, people who are new to their role, or teams that need help learning to function effectively and be productive.

"Our purpose is to help incorporate, no pun intended, listening skills throughout the organization beginning with you as the CEO. We want to ensure that all employees, clients, and stakeholders feel heard because SpecialMe.org is known as a listening organization with defined values that are practiced daily. Have we thrown too much at you?"

Jamie took a deep breath and sat back. As she did, she glanced at her watch and saw that she had about a minute left with Liam and Maria. "I think I'm good. This is going to take some getting used to. I thought I understood what I needed to do in the new role based upon what I had done at my previous job."

Maria commented, "We think it's important to recognize the skills, knowledge, and institutional awareness you bring to your new position. You don't have to let go of all of it. As a matter of fact, you shouldn't. It's too valuable and probably one of the reasons you were hired. As we go through this process, we hope you'll recognize what you need to keep, where you need to change—yes, change—and how you can adapt without losing who you are at your core and maintaining your personal values."

"Okay. I understand. I also see that we're at the top of the hour. I do have to leave. Meetings, you know," Jamie smiled as she stood up. "Thank you for working with me. I really appreciate this."

"You bet," Liam smiled broadly.

"See you next month." Jamie turned to leave and noticed that Liam and Maria sat back down. She couldn't wait to continue the conversation.

Creativity allows us to leave parts of our experiences and our heart with those on the receiving end. And whether it's now, or long after we've left this planet, I believe there's a reason for it all.

Quincy Jones, Music Producer

CHAPTER SEVEN
The Value of Establishing Values

Francis met Jaime at the door. There was an emergency that needed to be addressed. She ushered Jaime to the conference room. As soon as the door swung open there was a rousing *Surprise!* Jaime was confused and turned to look at Francis.

"We knew this would be your reaction," she laughed heartily.

"What is going on? It's not my birthday."

"Oh, we know. But here, we celebrate the little things. It's in our DNA, a core value. We want to celebrate your being here and let you know how much we appreciate you."

Jaime blushed. No one, not even at her previous job, had celebrated her. She was always the one who did something like this. "I don't know what to say. This has never happened for me before."

Mitchell piped up, "Jaime, we want you to know what a great job you're doin'. We recognize that our little comp'ny does things in a different way than what you're used to. But we appreciate how far you've come in a short 'mount a time. We can't wait to see what the next year will bring."

This was all a little overwhelming. Jaime could see Kristina, Larry, and Kristofer on the screen smiling and clapping. This was surreal. What kind of company does this? She had to admit to herself how uncomfortable this made her. Wasn't it her responsibility to plan surprises like this as the CEO? Especially the CEO of such a small company? She had mixed feelings but smiled, laughed, and enjoyed the cake and company.

In their office, Francis opened the conversation. "You're not used to this are you?"

"Not at all," Jaime admitted with a sigh of relief.

"It's okay. You'll get used to it. When Mitchell, Katrina, and I started the company we wanted to be sure nothing was held on to too tightly by us. We want everyone who works here to feel like they can plan something like what we just did and see it through. We sat down over the course of a weekend and hashed out our values, both personal and for the business. Celebrating the small wins or milestones is one of them."

"Interesting. Well, thank you. I'm honored," her reply was a little tongue in cheek as she thought about how she would be able to contribute to the values of the company.

One month later she was sitting at the museum café with Maria. They were waiting for Liam and had a nice chat about shoes. Maria, apparently, always dreamed of wearing four-inch heels. Jaime couldn't help but encourage her to go for it and not worry about what other people would think.

Liam arrived and apologized for being late. In one hand he held a book. In the other, a violin case. "It's a viola. A little larger than a violin. One of my orchestra members asked me if I could fix it. He seems to think there is something wrong with the sound that emanates," Liam shook his head. "Youth can be so hard on themselves, especially those who are driven by perfectionism. It's a challenge.

"Let's jump right in, okay? Tell us what you thought about L.I.S.T.E.N.—Values and what has happened at work," Liam said.

"Well, I find the way you have defined the values to be interesting. Wait, hold on. Are you the youth orchestra conductor at the conservatory?" Liam smiled and nodded. "Now I know where I've seen you. We attended a concert there a while ago. It was fabulous! Thanks for what you are doing.

"Back to the topic at hand. The company is very focused and uses inclusive language. And this brings me to my latest experience at work." Jaime told them about the surprise celebration and her conversation with Francis. "I couldn't help but wonder if the company has room for me to add to the values the founders have defined. I appreciate what I've experienced but must admit I feel like a third wheel and feel like I must adapt to what currently exists. It's a little frustrating. I want to contribute and be a part of the team. I'm not feeling it right now."

"Let me tackle this one, Maria, okay?"

"Oh yeah. Not a problem." She knew where he was going.

"Let's talk about the creative process, the creative mind. Believe it or not, many people think because I'm surrounded by musicians, I'm always encountering creative thinking. While there is some truth to that, there's also the other side of the brain that needs to be considered. Quincy Jones in his book *12 Notes on Life and Creativity* calls for sharpening your left brain. Now, where you work, many would assume that you are surrounded by left-brain leaning techies. Some may argue that they need to sharpen their right brain.

"What I propose to you is that the people in each group have the capacity to be both creative and analytical. The creatives I work with express it through music. They play instruments, write, conduct, and some even produce other musicians. With today's technology, that's not a hard thing to do for young people. This brings me to my point about being analytical. Today's technology insists that musicians who choose to move into the realm of conducting and producing music understand how to use the hardware and software produced by people like those who work at SpecialMe.org.

"Now, at SpecialMe.org the ability to focus and develop code is complemented by a person's ability to see a need, create a code, and then share or sell the program or app. The creation of the code takes creativity. They must see the code, feel the rhythm and flow, tweak their instruments, the 1's and 0's, and put it all together on the industry's equivalent to sheet music. Is this making sense?"

"Not really but keep going."

"Okay, this is where Maria comes in."

"As the CEO, the orchestra conductor, at SpecialMe.org it's up to you to share the creative aspects exhibited by so-called techies. They each have it inside of them, but it is rarely expressed. Some of it is an actual inability to do so, that's just the way some people are wired. But some of it is also because of a definition of who and how they should be according to the rest of the world because of what they do. Yes, writing code is very much a left-brain exercise. And when you do this all day long, sometimes it's easy to forget you are also a creative person.

"What it sounds like is the founders have discovered a way for those who are writing code or solving technical problems all day to let loose and express their creative side. And they have chosen to codify, sorry for the similar language, this *need* as an organizational value."

Jaime sat deep in thought as Liam and Maria waited patiently for her to speak.

"I'm not buying it. Plus, it doesn't answer my concern that there is no room for me to add what I think should be part of the values of the organization."

"Okay, Jaime. Tell us, what are the values at SpecialMe.org?"

Jaime was awkwardly silent. "I don't know."

Liam responded, "This might be something you need to remedy. What do you think? It's hard to speak about something you know nothing about. You've told us about conversations with Francis when she declared an organizational value. Not all values are expressed. There are many that are embodied and not written down. Does SpecialMe.org have written values for the public to see?"

Again, Jaime responded with, "I don't know." This was hard for Jaime. She prided herself on knowing all there was to know about her last company. But now she sat here in front of her Listeners admitting she did not know, of all things, expressed public values of her current employer where she is the CEO.

"You're not the first person we've met who doesn't know their company's values," Maria tried to comfort Jaime, to no avail. "Some have come to us from companies that've never defined their values. It might be worth considering asking where the values are written so you can read them. If they are not readily available for all to read—those who visit the website, walk into the office, or read your brochures—then this might be a point of entry for you to contribute your ideas."

Jaime sat silently. Maria and Liam waited.

"Okay. Let me think this one through. But I can say I recognize two of your values in practice, Luminaries and Excellence. You have shined light in an area I couldn't see and have moved me toward excellence by helping me learn and grow. I think my next step will be to let my guard down, and my pride, and ask the founders about this."

They parted ways and this time Jaime stayed at the cafe. She took out a notebook and jotted down some thoughts and some personal values. Some she'll discuss with the founders and others with Freddy.

There is no normal life that is free of pain. It's the very wrestling with our problems that can be the impetus for our growth.

Fred Rogers

CHAPTER EIGHT

The Value of Friendship and Frank Conversations

If you can't trust a friend to pull you up out of a rut, who can you trust?

It had been about a week since Jaime last met with her Listeners. She was still mulling over their conversation when the phone rang.

"Hello, friend!"

"Hi!" A familiar and welcome voice greeted her today.

"Whatcha up to?"

"Oh, you know, saving the world once again," Jaime laughed, feeling the tension leave her shoulders.

"Do ya wanna meet for lunch tomorrow? I just had a client cancel."

"Hang on. Let me check my calendar." Jaime set the phone down and opened her spiralbound calendar. "You're in luck. I have about an hour and a half free at one o'clock. Will that work?"

"Sure will. Best part about owning my own biz. I can move things around if I need to. But tomorrow, the person who canceled was my last appointment for the day. How 'bout Leo's? I can go for a chicken salad sandwich. Have been craving it for a few days."

Jaime laughed at her friend who always seemed to be craving some kind of food or drink. Since Lenora swore off alcohol, Jaime knew they would be heading to a place that was all natural, local, and ethically sourced. *Farm to Table* was one of her mottos and she made every effort to adhere to her principles. Online shopping was a rare occurrence.

It took Lenora years to realize her vision, dream, and define her personal values which she then wove into the fabric of her business.

As a bespoke tailor, she was a creative person who coached men and women to become the best version of themselves. She made every effort to source fabric from local artisans, trying to exhaust every possible option before going out of state and then internationally. She visited each artisan in person, each factory in the country and internationally, and researched how employees were treated, as well as the supply chain and transport system before she signed an agreement. Jaime was amazed by her friend's commitment to this process and credited her success to her well-established practice.

They met at the entrance to Leo's the next day and hugged like they had not seen each other in years instead of one week. "You look fabulous," gushed Lenora as she admired Jaime's outfit. Of course, it just happened to be one she created for her best friend.

"I know! Let me know if you want to meet the person who made it for me." They laughed and went in.

"Busier than usual," commented Lenora.

"Yes, it is. Hey, I want to have a serious conversation with you. Stop laughing," Jaime lightly tapped her friend's hand and continued. "I've had a conversation with my Listeners about values. I don't know why I didn't think about talking to you about this. You've incorporated a value system into your business like it was second nature."

"Yep. You're right. I'm perfect. Defining my values came to me like a lightning bolt and I've been able to magically incorporate them into my whole life." Lenora gave her friend a sly look and then couldn't help herself. She laughed out loud at Jaime's serious reaction. "I'm just joking. Lighten up, Jaime. Good golly."

Jaime was visibly embarrassed, and Lenora stopped laughing as quickly as she started.

"Oh my gosh. You're serious about this, aren't you?"

Wiping the lone tear from her cheek, Jaime nodded. "I know this may sound crazy, but I'm struggling. I know I have values. I know I have practiced them. But SpecialMe.org embodies their values like it's second nature. I have never experienced this and just need to talk with the person I know who has the same approach in their business and in life." Jaime continued speaking, reverting to Italian.

Lenora let her finish. "Okay, friend. I know you know I don't speak I-talian. Let's start where you stopped speaking English.

"First, you're right, I practice my values daily and I made sure they are incorporated into the daily work at the office with everyone who is there. But this didn't happen overnight. It's a daily conscious effort that only looks second nature.

"I credit my Pops and Mom with instilling in me a strong work ethic. I credit my English teacher with helping me find my voice. And, lastly, I continued to develop my values and work ethic by following entrepreneurs, in both the private and public world, corporate and nonprofit, who were creators, inventors, investors, philanthropists, and thought leaders who saw a need and found a way to help.

"Remember when I took two years off to travel?"

Jaime nodded and smiled.

"Well, that was more than a spiritual journey in my mid-twenties. I sat down with my parents and told them why I wanted to take two years to travel. Explaining *why* was the only way I knew I'd get their support. They taught me that I don't have to have all the answers to pursue a dream. But I do need to understand, even at the simplest level, why I want to go for it. This forced me to do some research.

"Then I reread some of my journals. Throughout the years I had developed a heart for those in dire conditions. I wrote about it more than I thought. My journals were not about me. They were about everyone I encountered.

"Next, I thought about school. I wasn't too hip on school, if you remember. All I wanted to do was sew and draw. I had to convince my parents that school was not right for me. They pushed back but I stood my ground.

"Finally, after months of planning, and dropping out of school, I started my journey. I kept thinking about the author Elizabeth Gilbert," Lenora laughed. She paused her story when their food arrived. After thanking the server, which she always does, the story continued.

"You know from the letters and postcards I sent you the transformation I had. Elizabeth Gilbert was one of my inspirations. Writing was my conduit, but fabric and fashion were my passions. As I went through those two years and saw how life is in other countries, especially those where a lot of clothing is manufactured and fabric is exported, my vision for my business began to reveal itself."

Jaime was listening with her whole body. She ate, nodded her head, ate, and interjected a question where it seemed there was a break in the story.

"Jaime, sometimes the values of a business are baked in only after years of trial and error or life experiences. It sounds to me like SpecialMe.org has both perspectives. Practicing their values comes naturally because they have been living them. They may have defined them, but I guarantee you that defining them was not easy, because having values to guide them personally is part of their DNA."

"Well, I have values too. Why does it feel like they're not part of my DNA?"

"But they are. You simply haven't had to speak truth to life. You haven't had to write out your values. Do you recognize some of your personal values in the organization?"

"Yes, however, it feels awkward. It's a little discombobulating."

"Wow! I see you have been using that word-a-day calendar I gave you for Christmas," Lenora teased.

Jaime laughed, "I've been waiting for the perfect time to use it."

They laughed and ordered dessert and coffee to go. Time was running short.

"I don't like feeling confused, but I am beginning to understand where the founders of SpecialMe.org are coming from. I did recognize their values when I went through the interview process, and it was one of the reasons I wanted the job. Why do I feel like I have to change the organization or contribute my own ideas?"

"Well, let me respond with two questions. Why do you think the organization needs to be changed? And, what's wrong with contributing your own ideas?"

Jaime had to leave the conversation there. It was time to leave so she wouldn't be late for her next appointment. "Thanks, Lenora. Our conversations always help. I'll let you know what's going on next week."

Let me win, but if I cannot win, let me be brave at the attempt.

Special Olympics, Athlete Oath

CHAPTER NINE
Values in Action

Jaime sat in the front seat, trying to relax. She had met with Liam and Maria for the past two months and discussed the values their organization had incorporated and how they put them into practice. Today she, along with Freddy and Luna, were on the way to an event for athletes with special needs that SpecialMe.org supports. She would see first-hand one of the values she discussed with Francis being put into action.

SpecialMe.org has been committed from the start to helping people with learning and physical challenges. They support local sporting events specifically focused on ensuring all who want to participate in sports can participate. The other program they support is music therapy, which turned out to be why Liam knew about their organization.

"I don't know why I'm so uncomfortable. I've heard about this event since I started. They told me that business is intentionally slow at this time of year so all the employees can participate. In addition, though not with as much dedicated time and resources, each of us can bring to the table a worthy cause or organization that needs support. SpecialMe.org will consider each and decide, as a team, the merits of supporting events or nonprofits.

"We make sure the event or nonprofit aligns with our values and mission and that our resources, which can be financial or time working directly with the organization, affect the population in need and make the world a better place for them."

"Okay. What's wrong with that?" Freddy asked in Italian.

Jaime didn't miss a beat responding in her native language. "Nothing. Seriously, I know this is a good thing. I think what I'm uncomfortable with is . . ." She hesitated before continuing. "I don't know how to act with the athletes and their families. I've never experienced this." Her face was flushed with embarrassment, and she shifted more than seemed reasonable in her seat.

Freddy didn't respond. He just waited for her to process what was expressed. A vulnerability.

"Mama," Luna started in Italian, "What do you mean? Where are we going? What kind of people are you talking about?" There was a slight presence of fear in her question.

Jaime shifted in her seat to face Luna. "No, *piccola mia*. What I mean is, we are going to meet new people who will be very nice but may not speak the way we do or walk like us and be different in ways we aren't used to seeing. We may feel uncomfortable but it's important for us to be polite. *Capisci?*"

"*Capisco*. Will we see people like Caroline?"

"Who is Caroline?"

"She's in my class. She can't walk and has to use a wheelchair."

"Yes, Luna, we will most likely see people like Caroline. You see, already you know more than I do." Jaime smiled and touched her daughter's hand as Luna smiled and looked out the window.

"I can't wait! Caroline is really nice and funny!"

Luna's excitement was infectious and calming. What Jaime was recognizing in herself had more to do with her preconceived notions of what she would experience than it had to do with the reality of the event SpecialMe.org intentionally supports.

Once they arrived Francis met them at the entrance where she was helping athletes and families navigate where they needed to go. "Hi! So happy to see you. Finally, I get to meet your family." Instead of shaking hands, Francis pulled first Freddy then Luna in for a bear hug. She was very much a hugger. "Are you ready for an adventure?" she asked Luna.

Luna was jumping up and down anxious to help. "I'm hoping to see Caroline. She's a girl in my class. She's in a wheelchair."

Francis smiled and asked if Luna knew Caroline's last name. "I don't remember," Luna admitted. "But maybe I'll still see her, then I can ask."

"You are absolutely right! I love your positive attitude," Francis could not help but jump up and down with Luna. Then she took her hand and reassured Freddy and Jaime that Luna would be fine. "Enjoy yourselves. Get to know the athletes. Mitchell and the gang are all here. It's the only time of the year we get to see Katrina, Kristofer, and Larry in person." With that, Francis and Luna skipped off to see if they could find Caroline.

Freddy took Jamie's elbow, and they started walking. Jaime felt a calmness envelope her fears and wanted to skip along from location to location just like Luna. "This is going to be a beautiful experience. Just like my Listeners expressed as one of their core values, Service, I can now understand it."

The competition was amazing. Everywhere they went positive energy exploded from the athletes and their families. No one was worried about failing. They only encouraged the athletes to be brave, to try, and to celebrate all the small victories. But there was no shortage of competitive spirit amongst the athletes. The event was surrounded by a positive glow for all who participated. Even though she had never experienced being around people with special needs, this was a life-altering day for Jaime. A true shift in her way of thinking, listening, and celebrating life.

She always considered herself to be an encourager. But this was different. What she experienced were fearless people confronted daily with great challenges. It wasn't the athletes she observed this in, it was their families, friends, and other supporters. She experienced families who understood the need to be authentic and positive even amid what must be days filled with worry, exhaustion, frustration, and above all else, unconditional love for their athletes.

This was a true exercise in activating your values. When values become a part of your day-to-day way of being, it is not necessary to express them verbatim. They are expressed through action. SpecialMe.org explained their value for human dignity through their actions.

On the way home Luna rattled off all she experienced and all the athletes she met. Her event program was covered with the unique signatures of the athletes who happily signed it. "I can't wait to do this again next year!"

Freddy and Jaime chuckled and shared their experience with Luna and then with each other after Luna finally fell asleep. "I would have never done this on my own," Jaime admitted.

"Neither would I," Freddy said. "That was a little overwhelming, but not in the way I anticipated. It was such a joyful experience."

"I agree," Jaime took his hand in hers and they drove the rest of the way home in silence.

[Odysseus]. . . found that the first task of transition was unlearning, not learning anew. . . [In] order to change—really change, and not just to switch positions—you must realize that some significant part of your old reality was in your head, not out there.

William Bridges, Author, *Transitions: Making Sense of Life's Changes*

CHAPTER TEN

When Values Need to be Recognized, Defined, and Embodied

Jaime was anxious to meet with Liam and Maria the week following the event SpecialMe.org sponsored. This time they met at the local library in one of the meeting rooms. Liam explained they needed to plan for two hours. It was time to talk about the values at SpecialMe. org and Jaime's personal values.

"It's so great to see you. I hope everything at work is going well," Liam started.

"It's fantastic! We sponsored an event that supports people with special abilities. Funny, in the past I would have said people with disabilities. What I came to realize is that everyone is special— no pun intended. We all have gifts and talents that should be valued no matter how simple or presumably benign.

"I had to face my own prejudices and ignorance at this event. It wasn't only about those with special abilities, but also about their family and friends who support them. To top it off, many of my misconceptions about SpecialMe.org were dispelled. I was challenged by being confronted with a community I had only seen, in all honesty, through pictures and on TV.

"It's a little embarrassing to admit. I thought I was a compassionate and aware person. It turns out, I'm not flawless." Jaime punctuated her final statement and was completely sincere about her self-evaluation and revelation. No tears welled up in her eyes. She was completely matter of fact and chose to expose her vulnerability without getting emotional.

"Whoa! Didn't expect to hear all of that," chimed Maria, not trying to conceal her surprise.

Liam smiled and leaned back in his chair while Jaime shared how she experienced the day and what happened that night at home.

"When we arrived home, Freddy and I were up until well past midnight talking about the day, our family, our marriage, and how amazing our daughter is. She didn't blink with fear the whole day. She jumped in and did all she could to help others. She had a genuine desire to get to know everyone and hear their stories. We had to admit that the two of us were more guarded and, though it was a beautiful experience, found it difficult to fully relax. This was something we had never encountered.

"We talked about the values the two of you have shared with me from your organization: Luminaries, Impassioned, Service, Teamwork, Excellence, and Notice. Then we talked about the values of SpecialMe.org. I finally had a conversation with Francis. She explained that their values are simple, and they also use an acronym: ACT&ASK. *Aware. Collaborative. Trustworthy. Attentive. Supportive. Kind.* Simple, right?"

Maria and Liam nodded in agreement.

Jaime continued, "Well, I must admit that I didn't feel that way at first. I thought it was too simple. I pushed back, trying to assert my own ideas into the discussion. Francis, just as I used to do with my old boss, listened attentively. Did you catch that?"

Jaime shook her head and frowned. "It took me a while to catch on that she was implementing L.I.S.T.E.N. while also embodying one of SpecialMe.org's values." Jaime paused here, opening the door for discussion.

"Wow, again," Maria leaned forward as she spoke. "Can I ask you something?"

"Sure."

"What have you learned about your leadership style?"

Jaime looked a little taken aback as the two women locked eyes. She squirmed in her seat like a child in school who was caught cheating. Then she glanced at Liam hoping he would assist. Instead, she saw that he too was leaning in waiting to hear her response. It took a few seconds, which felt like minutes, for Jaime to respond.

"Well, I've always prided myself as a person who took the time to get to know people. You know, get to know their backstory. Then I always followed up and, I think, made them feel special. I did that as a person who earned my position. As in an orchestra, I sat in the second chair and supported the first violin. But now, here I am in the first chair and I'm finding it difficult to be who I was. Why is that?" Jaime whispered her question and looked away in deep thought.

The three of them sat in silence. At this point, it was the best tactic for Liam and Maria. They could tell that Jaime was at a crossroads in her development. She had to accept that she still had the qualities of the person she used to be but not the same responsibilities. Her role had changed. Did she have to change with it?

That is the question she asked Liam and Maria. "I know who I am at my core. I know how I like to function at work, in my community, and at home. I'm a helper, a problem solver. People feel comfortable coming to me with their concerns. As for your question about who I am as a leader, my leadership style. Honestly, I'm not sure."

"Okay. Is it alright if I interject here?" Maria asked.

With a nod from Jaime, she continued. "I have had to redefine my role several times. In middle school, I had to choose between joining sports teams, which was expected since my family is very athletic, or going to the computer lab. I chose the computer lab and that set me apart from my family and some of my friends. In high school, I had to choose between working on my skills as a programmer and meeting with my teacher every day after school or finding a part-time job. I chose to develop my skills. That set me apart from my friends who were all working and buying the latest of everything.

"Then, after developing the first app with my teacher, I had to decide if I would be a part of the team and start our company or enjoy my final two years of high school. I chose the company which meant I had to grow up quickly and didn't get to do a lot of the things my peers were doing, like homecoming and prom. I didn't even date while I was in high school. And to close this story, before I graduated from high school, I had to decide whether to go on to college or continue as an entrepreneur. That was a little more difficult because of the need to be at the forefront of technology and software development. It made sense to go to college to learn from the professors there. So, I chose college.

"Big mistake. I discovered two things about myself. First, my practical experience was invaluable. Second, I didn't enjoy lectures. I had to make yet another decision. After one semester, I left college, started working from home, and enrolled in an online college program. I have an entrepreneur's heart and mind. My point here is to help you remember that transitions, the choice to move through these transitions and decide, are not easy and have rewards and consequences. For me to move forward, I had to learn to appreciate who I was to become who I am. Does this make sense?"

"Before you answer, let me chime in," said Liam. "Our purpose today is to help you navigate through your experience at the event. To help you define your values, both personal and professional, so that you can align with SpecialMe.org. To do this, especially as a new leader, a new CEO, you must examine where you've been so you can define where you'll go."

"I get it," Jaime nodded. "I wasn't as exposed as a leader at my previous job. Here, not only am I exposed but the team is smaller and more collaborative. They are always in conversation with each other. Nothing is a secret. Being open is encouraged. It does make me uncomfortable, but I think I understand why.

"Freddy and I did discuss our family and our values. We had a difficult time expressing them even though we knew what they were. Make sense?"

Liam and Maria agreed and encouraged Jaime to continue.

"Hmm. Well, maybe I didn't explain that well. To get to the point, we finally wrote out our values and put them on the refrigerator. The next morning, we explained to Luna what it meant. She still has a lot to learn, and we will continue to develop all of this for our family.

"Then at work, Francis explained ACT&ASK to me. This is where my learning to define who I am as a leader in this organization comes into play. Like you said, Maria, I'm in transition. What our time together today has revealed is that as a leader, I have to be open to having the support of a person who is technically my subordinate, even though she is one of the founders. But in practice and in alignment with SpecialMe.org's values, she and I are peers. I need to learn how to allow her to be my sounding board and to teach me lessons about leadership."

"Yes, yes," Liam clapped his hands and moved to the edge of his seat. "That's moving in the right direction. Leadership isn't always top-down. As you did at your old job and what Francis is doing for you now, leading occurs from the bottom-up, too. We refer to it as leading from the bottom of the pyramid. Flattening the organization with an understanding that decision makers still exist but communication within the organization is inclusive, encouraged, and expected."

"Okay. I'm getting it. But what about values?"

"It's important for organizations to have guiding principles. Values, if you will. This helps in many ways. One of which is decision making. Let me give you an example. I had to make a change in the orchestra last year. Since I work with youth, it can be a sensitive thing to do. Our first chair, designated to a violinist in this case, so you know which role I'm talking about. Well, she was aging out of our orchestra. We had to replace her. One of our values is to recognize talent within. How we define that has more to do with talent within an individual than seeking talent that exists within the current orchestra.

"So, when it came time to start the auditions, it was easy to explain why the person currently occupying the second chair would also have to go through the procedure of auditioning. It was also easy, and accepted, that auditions would be open to the public. We communicate and put into practice our values daily. The members of the orchestra and their parents, who are a very important component of our organization, all know our values. It alleviates tension, resentment, rumors, and anxiety."

"Okay, okay. This is sinking in. So, ACT&ASK isn't as simplistic as I thought. My personal values need to align with SpecialMe.org or any other organization. I don't necessarily have to change but maybe adapting is a better way of approaching this. Adapt and learn. Finally, there's the matter of discovering my leadership style."

"Yes," piped in Maria. "With transitions comes an opportunity for reflection and you can either maintain, adapt, or redefine who you are as a leader. Self-evaluation and transitioning to a new role don't mean you have no influence or that you must change who you are at your core. It simply reinforces the need to establish and embody personal values as guiding principles to help you through the process. And then align with and contribute to the values espoused by the new, or transforming, organization."

With that, their time expired. They agreed on the next location and time and left the library.

When Leonard Bernstein, the famous orchestra conductor, was asked about the most difficult instrument to play, he surprised many by saying it was the second violin. "I can get plenty of first violinists, but to find one who plays second violin with as much enthusiasm, or second French horn, or second flute, that's a problem. And yet if no one plays second, we have no harmony."

As shared by Marriage Missions International, "Quotes on 'Communication Tools'"

CHAPTER ELEVEN
A Conversation with Francis

Jaime arrived at the office early. Even the metro was a little quiet and the walk to the office was unfamiliar since few people occupied the sidewalk. It had been almost a year since she started at SpecialMe. org. Her time with Liam and Maria had opened the possibilities hidden in the position of CEO and helped her understand how to negotiate relationships, communication, and growth.

Today she had an afternoon set aside to meet with Francis who had become a confidante, mentor, and good friend. This was an opportunity to discuss the previous year and how to move forward. Together they would shape the strategy session that was scheduled for the following week.

But there was more that Jaime wanted to discuss. She wanted to understand how Francis moved from being the go-to person to the fulltime role of COO and, in the vernacular of an orchestra, second chair. She wanted to know if this was a conscious decision and how they could continue to move forward on the amicable path they had created.

To her surprise, she wasn't the first one in the office. Mitchell had already been there for at least an hour. He took a break when she arrived, and they enjoyed a cup of tea and light conversation. She was comforted by the easy demeanor of this man. His 6'5" stature misrepresented his gentle, caring nature. He laughed easily and always had a good story to tell or a joke to share. Jaime had a great appreciation for his gifts.

They were holding their stomachs, heads thrown back, bellowing with laughter when Francis arrived.

"Mitchell is the best storyteller," Jaime proclaimed in between breaths. "This is one of my favorite times of the day, hearing a good story or joke. I wish I had your gift," she addressed Mitchell with authentic admiration. He simply smiled, patted her hand, waved hello to Francis and went back to work.

"It's so easy to forget how important daily humor is, and a good belly laugh. Don't you think?" Jaime was following Francis to their shared office.

"Mitchell has had me rolling on the floor so many times. Now you know what a gift he is."

Jaime wiped the mascara from underneath her eyes and cheeks and reapplied her signature look. Not a hair out of place, 4-inch heels to match the outfit, and perfectly applied cosmetics. Francis admired her friend and her ability to stay true to who she is at heart. Over the course of the last year, she had plenty of opportunities to try to change her, but it was a wasted effort. Thankfully.

"Shall we go to the café?" Jaime asked.

"I have a surprise. There's a new place and it's right downstairs. Did you see the food truck? I thought we could grab something and work here."

"Perfect. More comfortable. What kind of food?"

"Breakfast, European style," Francis replied with a twinkle in her eye.

They made their way to the food truck and back to the office just as quickly. The breakfast wasn't traditionally Italian. It was German and fantastic. They ate in silence as they started their morning routine by checking their email.

That afternoon they walked into the conference room ready to tackle the agenda. "Before we start, can I ask you a question?"

Jaime wanted to be sure she didn't miss an opportunity to learn a little more about her office mate.

"Of course. What's up?"

"I just want to understand how you have experienced the past year. You went from essentially being the CEO, even with Mitchell and Katrina in their roles, to the COO when I came on board. Was that deliberate? Would you share that with me?"

"That's an interesting question and not one I was expecting. Hmm . . . Let me think about that for a minute." Francis took a seat and stared through the glass wall that separated the conference room from all the other offices in the shared workspace. She took her time before responding.

"Okay. We're sitting in a cone of trust, right?"

Jaime nodded in agreement.

"Fine. The decision to find a CEO was not one that was supported by all. Some had reservations about bringing a new person on board. I never expressed my opinion but. . . in fairness to the question you asked, I was also skeptical, even though I'm the one who suggested it. I had settled into my role, or roles, in a startup and thought my way of functioning was adequate. Our business was thriving and there didn't seem to be a need to change. So, the decision was not mine, but I agreed, nonetheless.

"When you first arrived, it was a little hard to give up control. Harder than I had imagined it would be. Plus, you had a steep learning curve and we all agreed I would be your tutor and mentor. Your energy during the interview was dynamic and your credentials were outstanding. I must admit, I was a little intimidated.

"But then we started working together. The first few months were great, but we all got a little too comfortable. When you started your regular meetings with your Listeners, there was a shift in your approach, demeanor, and enthusiasm. You started asking me questions. I felt needed and appreciated for my knowledge and expertise.

"Age was definitely a factor in my way of thinking. I didn't want you to think I was too young to know what I was talking about. I have worked hard to help develop the company and gain the trust of our customers and employees. Then my role shifted to a supporting one and I was uncomfortable. But what I came to realize was that you were willing to listen, engage, learn, and become a part of the team."

Jaime listened without interrupting even though so many questions were swirling in her mind. Listening was a part of who she was and how she wanted to be known as a leader. She gave colleagues and others the space to speak without interruption. Without offering a solution. Without judgment.

"What I had to learn," Francis continued, "was to become the person who sits in the second chair, to use your orchestra analogy. Was it an easy transition? No. But I am committed to SpecialMe. org and arrived at a place where I knew my role as COO was vital to ensuring our growth and effectiveness. So, here we are, both learning to be something we weren't in the past. What's remarkable is that we are both thriving. Don't you think so?"

Jaime took the time to be sure Francis was finished. Sitting back in her seat to gather her thoughts about how to respond, it came to her. She, Francis, and the team had created a new space to exist in harmony. "Yes, I agree wholeheartedly. The team is thriving, and I give credit to you. You serve as the person who makes sure the company runs smoothly while I fulfill my role. But we do this without being territorial. We don't work in silos. We share, all of us, we discuss, and we make things happen. It's really remarkable.

"I'm thinking about how far I have come and how comfortable, not in an unproductive way, I am here. We encourage each other to continue to grow and be creative. We function with our values as our guideposts. This was all a little foreign to me. But I'm glad I have experienced all of it."

They continued their conversation using up the remainder of time they had reserved. The strategy session would have to be postponed. Luckily, the conference room was available again the next day and they were able to reschedule the meetings they had on their calendars.

Someone To Tell It To has a vision to create a world in which Everyone matters and Everyone is recognized as having a voice that needs to be heard, and . . . Loneliness is diminished.

Tom Kaden and Michael Gingerich, Co-Founders of Someone To Tell It To

EPILOGUE

In the middle of the second year of Jaime's tenure as CEO, SpecialMe. org was gaining traction and attention from industry leaders. By the end of the second year, they had received two offers. One was to buy the business outright. The other was a proposed merger.

To everyone's surprise, Jaime asked Maria to serve as a consultant. As she had experienced in the past, everyone except Jaime questioned her qualifications. "She's so young," they would say. "There's no way she knows what she's talking about. What we do is hard to understand," they proclaimed.

Then Jamie suggested the team remember what was said about them when they were first starting. How many were judged and deemed incapable. "Remember the event we hosted last year? I was so nervous and didn't know what to expect. I arrived expecting to see a spectacle that would break my heart. Instead, what all of you and the athletes and their families taught me is to not judge others. Instead, let's practice our values. Be kind and listen."

Jamie had the advantage of knowing Maria's story. She couldn't help but smile broadly when Maria answered all the questions and assured the team that she would help them through the decision-making process. She would ensure that they would make the best decision for the company and each individually.

The team at SpecialMe.org had two weeks to decide. With Maria, they discussed their history, their values, and whether they were confident one of the two businesses would uphold their standards, appreciate their stakeholders, and something Maria brought up that they had not considered. Would the team stay together and run the business with some autonomy?

Together they reviewed each offer. They listened to each other's ideas, logic, dreams for the future if they sold, and the possibility to have greater impact with the resources of a larger organization if they merged. This was a taxing time for all of them since they had to continue to maintain their obligations to customers, manage personal needs and family dynamics, and think about their own future. What would it look like?

Jaime was able to maintain a neutral perspective. Even though she was now an integral part of the team, she didn't have the visceral reaction to the possibility of not having the business that Francis, Mitchell, and Katrina experienced as the founders.

Larry and Kristofer had their own concerns given their physical challenges. Working at SpecialMe.org was, well, special. There are not many businesses out there that not only see past their very public personal challenges, but even fewer that embrace who they are and the value they bring to building a business. Their fear seemed undeniably reasonable.

Two weeks went by quickly. Decision day arrived and Jaime and Francis were ready to discuss their counteroffer. In the end, they chose to merge with a company that aligned well with their mission, vision, and values. The condition of the merger was that the team would stay together for a minimum of three years to ensure a seamless transition and reassure current customers and other stakeholders that the new parent company valued each of them. Everyone would be able to work from their respective locations and they would be able to function with some autonomy as an entrepreneurial venture within the corporation.

To their delight, the company wanting to acquire SpecialMe. org agreed.

People are not machines.

Tom Kaden and Michael Gingerich

AFTERWORD FROM THE AUTHORS

Compassionate listening is fundamental to us. It is the driving force that informs our mission— To Help the World Listen. Compassion is a value that permeates Someone To Tell It To. It is woven into the fabric of who we are and why we exist. We model compassionate listening daily with every interaction we have.

Face-to-face interactions supersede engaging people with the assistance of technology. We are not opponents of technological progress by any stretch of the imagination. We would not be able to conduct business day in and day out without it. Technology is a fact of life. What we believe is that technology can become an excuse for not engaging another human being in-person. But people are not machines. People inherently crave and need connection with others. We embrace this guiding principle by practicing it daily when we, or our team members, meet with someone. Our team approach demonstrates to the person who needs someone to talk to that we value them, whether we meet them in person or virtually through technology. We recognize that everyone is of flesh and blood, a person with a pulse and emotions.

When we train at corporations, nonprofit organizations, and colleges or universities, or we are meeting with a leader at one of these organizations as part of their professional development, we not only share and practice our value of compassionate listening, but we also ensure the tool we use is one the trainees or the individual can practice and use.

In our book *Listening 2by2: A Paradigm Shift for Leaders (That's When the Magic Happens)* we describe the acronym L.I.S.T.E.N. This is the tool we put into practice and teach others to use. Included in this book is the explanation for L.I.S.T.E.N. We encourage you to read the book and then contact us if you want to learn more. We are always available to expound on L.I.S.T.E.N.'s meaning. We believe including compassionate listening in your leader's toolbox and practicing it organization-wide will produce a culture shift for you, personally, and for your organization.

Our podcasts demonstrate how we value and respect our guests. We prepare for the conversation by researching our guests, reading their books, and attending or viewing their presentations. We write questions that are on point to keep the conversation flowing with them. We ask, then we listen to our guests as they share their stories, advice, insight, and wisdom.

Each workday we put into practice the concept shared in this book—our **L.I.S.T.E.N.-Values** model (see the summary at the end of the book).

We consider it a privilege to serve as **LUMINARIES**–sources of light—for those who ask us to listen.

As a team, we move forward as **IMPASSIONED** listeners and trainers, improving our processes and strengthening bonds of friendship and camaraderie.

SERVICE is at our core. It is the heartbeat that ensures our values course through the veins of our system.

Stakeholders, defined as all who we encounter, ensure we move forward as a **TEAM**.

We pursue **EXCELLENCE** without constraining our ability to be a malleable entity that moves as one, releases what does not work, and absorbs concepts, procedures, and opportunities for a stronger organization.

We cannot become an effective team if we wear blinders. Our organization will falter, and our reach will shrink. We choose to remove blinders of doubt, prejudice, and judgment to **NOTICE** all the people we encounter, what is spoken and what is unspoken from them.

Our L.I.S.T.E.N.–Values concept was developed by our whole team. This is not the product of a top-down, adopt-or-leave approach to organization development. Our team listened, discussed ideas, debated, respected others' opinions, and crossed the finish line with our team intact, stronger, and our values defined.

We do not anticipate the values we have defined for our organization to be one size fits all and that therefore your organization should incorporate them verbatim. No, we believe it is important to develop personal and organizational values that are best suited for and support your defined purpose and mission.

It is important that as this process begins and unfolds, the team (or family or couple or community) understands the importance of compassionate listening. Respecting the input of others and finding balance in discussions that will lead to defined shared values is the objective.

If you do not know how to start, we can help. Our team is prepared to facilitate expressed, shared, and stakeholder-developed personal and/or organizational values.

The story we shared in this book only scratches the surface of leadership development, organization development, change management, and personal development. We are opening a conversation with you. Our intent is to demonstrate the challenges for a new leader and an organization during times of growth. We emphasize the importance of shared values at work and shared values at home. In many ways, they go hand-in-hand; they cannot be rigidly separated.

Developing shared values starts with a conversation. For the conversation to be meaningful, listening is key. Creating values within an organization (or conceivably within a family) the implementation of the values should not be top-down. Shared values are developed by including everyone who is being asked to embody and practice the values. Eventually, shared values will become a part of the DNA of an organization or a family.

Someone To Tell It To can facilitate this conversation. There will be times when our team members must interject in conversations to ensure the purpose of the training remains on target. However, our need to speak lessens as conversation amongst everyone increases because there is an increased atmosphere of trust and openness.

To learn more about how we can help, contact us at info@someonetotellitto.org. We and our team would be privileged to hear from you.

L.I.S.T.E.N. VALUES

Someone To Tell It To Values
WHAT WE ARE, STRIVE FOR, AND DO:

L I S T E N

LUMINARIES	**IMPASSIONED**	**SERVICE**	**TEAMWORK**	**EXCELLENCE**	**NOTICE**
We have a culture of compassion, care, concern, and support for everyone, that brings light to a sometimes dark world.	We are a team who sticks together to pursue a shared vision and purpose, and who seeks to achieve greatness together.	We are who we say we are and are consistent in providing excellent service.	We build relationships, communicate well and often, and create partnerships that are mutually beneficial.	There is always room to learn and grow.	We notice one another and let one another know they are valued.

- We know & respect each other
- We create an atmosphere of openness & vulnerability
- We spend time, energy, & resources on building our culture
- We don't forget the small things
- We have fun

- We achieve greatness by believing in our mission & by sweating & working hard to fulfill it
- "We" is greater than "me"
- We focus on the positive & keep moving forward

- We do our very best & let our best speak to the world's needs
- We are consistent so that others will be able to thrive & be well-served

- We are empathetic, gracious, & listen more than we speak
- We are honest & share openly & give & receive feedback sensitively & respectfully
- We model our listening skills & concepts effectively and compassionately

- We enable one another to do what is most life-giving & fulfilling within their roles & to support them in the aspects that are harder to embrace
- We strive to fine-tune our strengths & to recognize & acknowledge where we can be better
- We always have a reason to celebrate

- We listen & respond to what is spoken
- We pay attention to what is unspoken
- We affirm one another's personhood & respect them, offering affirmation, grace, & encouragement
- We pay attention to what is working well & to how we can improve to better fulfill the mission

> **"You need to be heard and valued as much as anyone else needs to be heard and valued."**
> *~ Listening 2by2: A Paradigm Shift for Leaders (That's When the Magic Happens!)*

L.I.S.T.E.N.

L - LEAN IN and REMOVE BARRIERS

- Eliminate distractions
- Look people in the eye
- Put technology away
- Encourage the introverts
- Remove barriers

I - INTERESTED and CURIOUS

- Be open to learning from everyone
- Invite others' ideas, visions, and dreams
- Acknowledge others' perspectives
- Ask probing questions
- Respond positively to others' input

S - SIMPLIFY and SELF-CARE

- Care for yourself
- Prioritize listening
- Delegate what others can do better than you
- Create intentional space to be fully engaged

T - TALK LESS and EMBRACE SILENCE

- Don't hijack conversations
- Don't jump in too fast
- Ask before offering your thoughts
- Hold back on judgments
- Do not try to fix everything
- Silence is revealing

E - EXPLAIN and ASK QUESTIONS

- Ask questions that solicit more than "yes" and "no" responses
- Ask questions to promote discovery and insight
- Convey support of and confidence in others
- Use "we" statements instead of "I" statements
- Avoid putting others on the defensive
- Use storytelling to clarify advice and answer questions

N - NEGOTIATE the WIN/WIN

- Listening is never done
- The goal of listening is to know and be known
- Listen from a place of humility
- Listening is intentional
- Listen for the *HOPE* that is unspoken
- Reveal the "larger picture" of the situation or issue at hand
- Be the Story Seeker

The Story Seeker's Listening Checklist

☐ Have I been listening twice as much as I've been speaking? At home? At the office? In meetings? Anywhere else relationships can be developed?

☐ What have been the barriers to listening well? How can I remove some of those barriers?

☐ Have I noticed a change in my relationships? If yes, how might I foster even greater depth in those relationships? If not, why not?

☐ Is technology becoming too much of a distraction to listen well? Do I need to set boundaries with emailing, social media, or entertainment so I can be more fully present?

☐ Have I been asking good questions of those around me with the goal of knowing them more and better? Do I need to set aside time with someone in particular to hear more from them?

☐ The most important time to listen is when you'd rather not. When conversations are hard, do I double-down on listening to help me understand another's perspective, or do I double-down on being right?

☐ Am I making space to listen to myself?

ABOUT THE AUTHORS

Michael Gingerich
Co-founder

Tom Kaden
Co-founder

Someone To Tell It To

Helping the World to Listen.

Michael and Tom are best friends, co-founders, and co-Chief Encouragement Officers of Someone To Tell It To, a Harrisburg, Pennsylvania-based nonprofit organization that cultivates meaningful relationships through compassionate listening and trains and educates others to do the same. Through Someone To Tell It To, Michael and Tom have helped lead more than 15,000 interactions of compassionate listening with people in the United States and in several countries around the world in the last 10 years.

In addition to being well-regarded experts in compassionate listening, Michael and Tom have launched and maintain their own successful podcast, the Someone To Tell It To podcast which has recorded more than 70 episodes. Having conducted scores of in-person and virtual workshops over the past few year for both corporate and nonprofit clients, Michael and Tom are highly-sought-after experts in topics that are timely and important.

Appearances:

   **Deloitte**

Available For: Keynotes | Podcasts | Webinars | Radio | Book Signings

Topics:
Compassionate Listening | Leadership
Team and Culture-Building

Titles:
· What is compassionate listening?
· The World's Need for Empathy & Compassion
· Effective Listening for Leaders and Teams
· Relationship Building in a Busy World

Latest Book:
Listening 2by2 :
A Paradigm Shift for
Leaders (That's When
the Magic Happens!)

amazon
★★★★★

Podcast:
Someone to Tell It
To Podcast
now on Season 5

Spotify

Apple Podcasts
Google Podcasts

To book Michael & Tom, or apply to be a podcast guest, email media@someonetotellitto.org

Acknowledgements

This book would not have been possible without the advocacy, diligence, and hard work of Isabelle Harman. Her vision and talent have enabled us to present a story of the truths we have learned throughout our years of listening with intention.

Someone To Tell It To is not possible nor a purveyor of hope without the vulnerability and trust given from those whose stories we and our teams of listeners have heard. Their stories are a gift to the world, helping all to learn to listen more deeply.

Most importantly, to our families, who have supported us unconditionally in the work we do. We owe everything to their belief in us and in the transformative power of ***listening***.

MORE BY:

TOM KADEN AND MICHAEL GINGERICH

Listening 2by2: A Paradigm Shift for Leaders (That's When the Magic Happens!) (2022)
Someone To Tell It To: Moved with Compassion (2017)
Someone To Tell It To: Sharing Life's Journey (2014)

TOM KADEN

CHAPTERS IN *CHICKEN SOUP FOR THE SOUL*

Chicken Soup for the Soul: The Power of Positive (2012) - "Uncovered"
Chicken Soup for the Soul: Angels Among Us (2013) - "Stranded"
Chicken Soup for the Soul: A Book of Christmas Miracles (2017) - "Stranded"

MICHAEL GINGERICH

A Light Shines in the Darkness (2011)

CHAPTERS IN *CHICKEN SOUP FOR THE SOUL*

Chicken Soup for the Soul: The Cancer Book (2009) - "Fear"
Chicken Soup for the Soul: Find your Happiness (2011) - "The Returning Light"
Chicken Soup for the Soul: Family Caregivers (2012) - "A Wonderful World?"
Chicken Soup for the Soul: Raising Kids on the Spectrum (2013) - "Obsession"

Made in the USA
Middletown, DE
09 October 2023